Endpapers *The European Cup squad of 1968. Back row (left to right): Bill Foulkes. John Aston, Jimmy Rimmer, Alex Stepney, Alan Gowling, David Herd. Middle row: David Sadler, Fred Owen (ticket manager), Tony Dunne, Shay Brennan, Pat Crerand, George Best, Francis Burns, Joe Armstrong (chief scout), Jack Crompton (trainer). Front row: Jimmy Ryan, Nobby Stiles, Denis Law, Matt Busby (manager), Bobby Charlton, Brian Kidd, John Fitzpatrick.*

UNITED
THE LEGENDARY YEARS
1958-1968

Best wishes

Denis Law

UNITED

THE LEGENDARY YEARS

1958-1968

DENIS LAW
and
PAT CRERAND

with Michael Leitch

RETRO CLASSICS
is a collection of facsimile reproductions
of popular bestsellers from the 1980s and 1990s

United: The Legendary Years 1958-1968 was first published in 1997
by Virgin Publishing

Re-issued in 2016 as a Retro Classic
by G2 Entertainment
in association with Lennard Books
Windmill Cottage
Mackerye End
Harpenden
Hertfordshire
AL5 5DR

ISBN 978-1-78281-280-7

Editor: Michael Leitch
Design consultants: Design 2 Print
Reproduction: The Colour Edge
Additional photography: Paul Atherton
Production consultants: Reynolds Clark Associates .

PICTURE ACKNOWLEDGEMENTS
The publishers and authors are grateful to the *Manchester Evening News*
and to Colorsport for providing most of the photographs which are not from
the authors' private collections. Thanks are also due to Sport & General,
Allsport and Getty Images for additional material.

A special thanks is due to Ray Adler who generously made available a number
of programmes and other items of memorabilia from his collection.

This book is a facsimile reproduction of the first edition of
United: The Legendary Years 1958-1968 which was a bestseller in 1997.
No attempt has been made to alter any of the wording
with the benefit of hindsight, or to update the book in any way.

CONTENTS

UNITED - A MAGIC CLUB

Of all the football clubs in Britain, Manchester United is the one most people would feel they had to include in their top-three list, if not their absolute choice for number one.

Since the Second World War this club has had a history like no other. Because of what happened at Munich, it is a history that no other club would knowingly wish on itself. But what United achieved in the decade after Munich almost defies explanation. And yet, history shows, it was somehow always likely to happen. The potential for greatness was never far away. It is equally true of today's team. That, to us, is what makes Manchester United a magic club.

United's huge power of attraction was as strong in the post-war years as it has ever been. Long before either of us came on the professional scene, the club had produced two fantastic teams. After he took over as manager in February 1945, Matt Busby – or Company Sergeant-Major Instructor Busby, as he was at first still known, the former Liverpool right-half and captain of Scotland – created the great Forties side. His captain was Johnny Carey at full-back, he had Jack Rowley and Stan Pearson scoring most of the goals, prompted by tricky runs and crosses from Charlie Mitten on the left wing.

Some well-known names in this forces team on its way to another match: (left to right) Frank Soo, Wally Barnes, Ted Drake, George Hardwick, unidentified, Neil Franklin, unidentified (half hidden), Raich Carter, Matt Busby, Stanley Matthews, Joe Mercer, Bernard Joy, Frank Swift (back to camera) and Jimmy Mullen.

UNITED THE LEGENDARY YEARS

In the next eleven seasons United were League Champions three times and runners-up four times. They won the FA Cup once, and were once losing finalists.

From 1951, beginning with the débuts of half-back Jackie Blanchflower (aged 18) and left-back Roger Byrne (21), Busby filtered his next generation of players into the side. These were the famous Busby Babes.

With his first blend of young and mature players Busby won the League in 1951-52, and over the next three years he brought more newcomers into the side – winger Johnny Berry, marksmen Tommy Taylor and Dennis Viollet, the brilliant wing-half Duncan Edwards, outside-left David Pegg, winger Albert Scanlon, centre-half Mark Jones, full-back Geoff Bent, midfielder Eddie Colman and inside-forwards Billy Whelan and Bobby Charlton, then more famous for being the nephew of Newcastle's Jackie Milburn. When they won the League in 1955-56, the average age of the side was 22.

Next in Matt Busby's sights was the European Cup, then about to enter its second season. The previous year, when Chelsea were League Champions, they had been heavily leaned on by the Football League not to take part, and had given in to the pressure.

Eddie Colman led the team that won the 1955 FA Youth Challenge Cup which also included Duncan Edwards, Shay Brennan, Wilf McGuinness and Bobby Charlton. The full line-up was: back row (left to right): Edwards, Beskett, Brennan, Hawksworth, Rhodes, Queenan. Front row: Jones, Fidler, Colman, McGuinness, Charlton

Busby, however, was determined to give his young team the chance to prove themselves against the Continent's top clubs. He won the necessary permission to take part and in 1956-57 United stormed to victory against Anderlecht, Borussia Dortmund and Atlético Bilbao before going down to the great Real Madrid side in the semi-final.

The following year United were again League Champions and swept through the first two rounds of the European Cup against Shamrock Rovers and Dukla Prague. Then came the two ties against Red Star Belgrade, which they won 5-4 on aggregate, booking themselves a second appearance in the semi-final.

On the way home from Belgrade after the second leg, their BEA Elizabethan aircraft touched down

Tommy Taylor (extreme right) and Dennis Viollet apply pressure in the Arsenal goalmouth at Highbury in February 1958, goalkeeper Jack Kelsey moves to save with support from Dennis Evans, while centre-half Jim Fotheringham looks on. This was the last league game before the European Cup match in Belgrade. **Below** *The wreckage of the BEA Elizabethan at Munich Airport.*

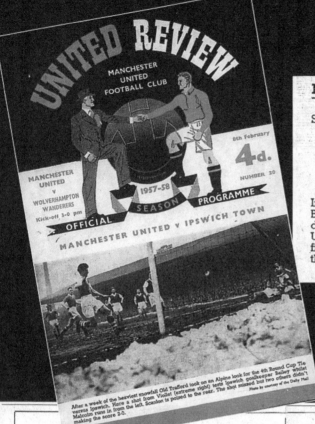

After a week of the heaviest snowfall Old Trafford took on an Alpine look for the 4th Round Cup Tie versus Ipswich. Here a shot from Viollet (extreme right) tests Ipswich goalkeeper Bailey whilst Malcolm runs in from the left. Scanlon is poised to the rear. The shot missed but two others didn't making the score 2-0.

Photo by courtesy of the Daily Mail

EUROPEAN CUP

Second round, second leg 5th February, 1958.

RED STAR BELGRADE
v.
MANCHESTER UNITED

In the capacity-packed football stadium in Belgrade 55,000 spectators watched United draw with the Red Stars by 3 goals apiece. United now proceed to the third round quarter finals for which pairings will be drawn within the next few days. Well done United!

The game that was would have been played at Old Trafford on the following Saturday — United were to entertain Billy Wright's Wolves. First copies of the programme were printed soon after the final whistle in Belgrade and before the news came through from Munich.

Next Home Match
F.A. CUP
United v.
SHEFFIELD W.
15 Feb. Kick-off 3-0 pm

Shirts Red

MANCHESTER UNITED
GREGG

Knickers White

Next Home Match
1st DIVISION
United v.
NOTTS. FOREST
22 Feb. Kick-off 3-0 pm

FOULKES 3   JONES 4   BYRNE

COLMAN 4   TAYLOR 9   EDWARDS 6

MORGANS 7   CHARLTON 8   VIOLLET 10   SCANLON 11

R   L

Referee:
A. E. Ellis, Halifax
Kick-off 3-0 pm

FOOTBALL GREEN PLEASE

Linesmen:
D. B. Hepworth, Sheffield
Red Flag
J. M. Jack, Halifax
Yellow Flag

L   R

MULLEN 11   MASON 10   MURRAY 9   BROADBENT 8   DEELEY 7

SLATER 6   WRIGHT 5   CLAMP 4

HARRIS 3   STUART 2

FINLAYSON 1
WOLVERHAMPTON W.

Team changes will be indicated by loudspeaker

Shirts Old Gold   Knickers Black

Team changes will be indicated by loudspeaker

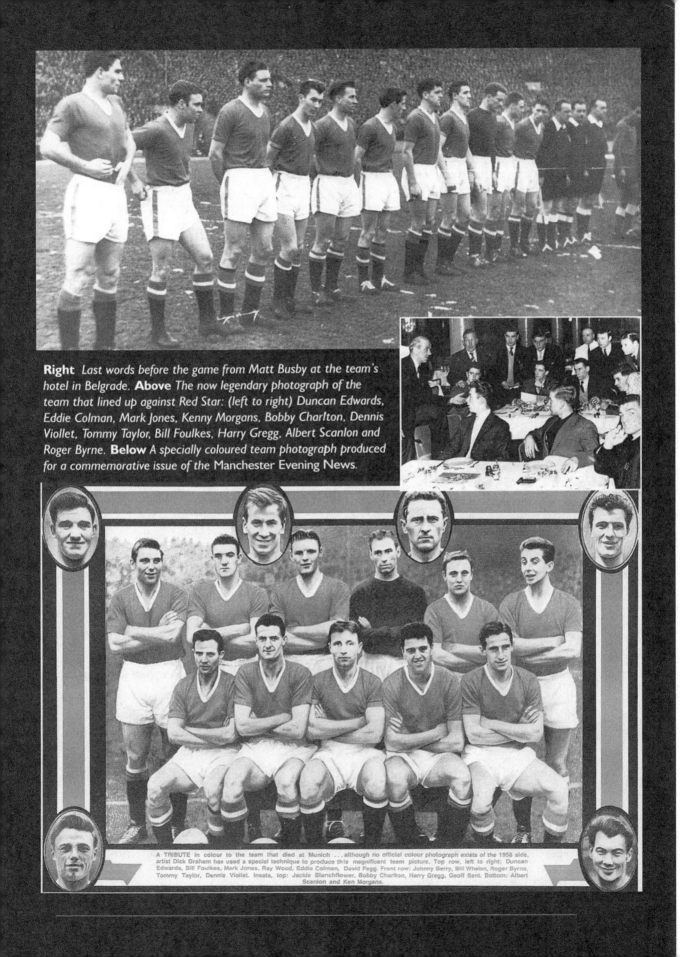

Right *Last words before the game from Matt Busby at the team's hotel in Belgrade.* **Above** *The now legendary photograph of the team that lined up against Red Star: (left to right) Duncan Edwards, Eddie Colman, Mark Jones, Kenny Morgans, Bobby Charlton, Dennis Viollet, Tommy Taylor, Bill Foulkes, Harry Gregg, Albert Scanlon and Roger Byrne.* **Below** *A specially coloured team photograph produced for a commemorative issue of the Manchester Evening News.*

A TRIBUTE in colour to the team that died at Munich ... although no official colour photograph exists of the 1958 side, artist Dick Graham has used a special technique to produce this magnificent team picture. Top row, left to right: Duncan Edwards, Bill Foulkes, Mark Jones, Ray Wood, Eddie Colman, David Pegg. Front row: Johnny Berry, Bill Whelan, Roger Byrne, Tommy Taylor, Dennis Viollet. Insets, top: Jackie Blanchflower, Bobby Charlton, Harry Gregg, Geoff Bent. Bottom: Albert Scanlon and Ken Morgans.

at Munich to refuel. Snow began to fall heavily and the pilot had severe difficulty in taking off again. Two attempts were aborted before he tried again for a third time. The plane failed to lift off and crashed just beyond the end of the runway.

Twenty-three people died. Of that brilliant generation of players United lost Roger Byrne, Duncan Edwards, Tommy Taylor, Eddie Colman, Mark Jones, Billy Whelan, Geoff Bent and David Pegg. Two survivors, Johnny Berry and Jackie Blanchflower, were badly injured and never played again. Matt Busby struggled on the edge for days before he at last began to recover.

When the news came out, it was not only the city of Manchester that went into mourning. The tragedy affected the entire nation. It later became one of those things that are forever fixed in your memory – knowing where you had been when you heard the news. These are our stories:

Pat Crerand: *In my Celtic days, tackling Willie Wallace of Hearts.*

Pat Crerand: I know exactly where I was. I was getting a trolley bus up to Glasgow Cross when I saw it on a big placard outside a shop where they sold papers: 'United in Plane Crash'.

I thought straight away, 'Well, the papers don't always tell the truth. They'll have just bumped into something, it's probably nothing.'

Then I got a train from Glasgow Cross to Celtic Park and there it was the only topic of conversation. It was about six o'clock in the evening. We didn't know any details, and the information was slow coming through .

I was still a young lad who had just signed for Celtic the year before, but we all knew about United and what a great team they had, with all those young players. Everybody knew Matt Busby as well, so it was a big shock to everyone in Glasgow when it happened.

Denis Law: I was in a wee café across the road from the Huddersfield Town ground. The news came through that there had been a plane crash in Munich and that Manchester United were involved. Some players had been killed but we didn't know who. Then we heard that Matt Busby had survived but was on the danger list. For everyone involved in the game those first days after the crash were something they'll never forget.

Denis Law: *In my first season for Huddersfield, and* **(below)** *United's game against Sheffield Wednesday, my first visit to Manchester and Old Trafford.*

It was strange, too, but for a lot of other people, not just in Britain but all over the world, this was the moment they began to take an interest in Manchester United. They heard about the crash and were moved by it. Even though they had no particular interest in football, all of a sudden here was a team that had lost more than half its members in an air disaster. And so they began to follow United, to see how they would pick themselves up and go on through the years.

The fact that many of the players who died were so young seemed to be an important part of it. Usually in football young players come into the first team in ones and twos. The Busby Babes were different. They were based around a side that had first come together some years before in the Youth eleven, and

when Matt Busby drafted them into the first team he did it at a speed which I think was unknown in football up till then.

Less than two weeks after the crash, United had to take the field again for a fifth-round FA Cup match against Sheffield Wednesday. It was a midweek game and I went over to Old Trafford with a friend of mine. We paid eight times the usual price of a ticket to get in, but we just had to be there.

The original match programme was printed before the news of the disaster came out, and had to be scrapped. When they printed it again, no-one knew who would be turning out for United. Their half of the sheet was left blank, with just dotted lines that spectators could fill in when they announced the side over the tannoy.

In the days leading up to the game Jimmy

Murphy, the assistant manager, was in charge of the team. He went into the transfer market and bought Ernie Taylor, a veteran international from Blackpool, and Stan Crowther from Aston Villa. Crowther was officially Cup-tied but the FA gave him a special dispensation to play in the match and he signed the transfer forms about an hour before the kick-off.

Also in the team was Alex Dawson, with whom I had played for Aberdeen Schoolboys Under-15 side, but he was the only player at the club I knew personally. The rest of the day was a complete first-time experience for me. Not only had I never played at Old Trafford, it was the first time I had ever been to Manchester.

Shay Brennan made his début and was United's star player. He was on the left wing instead of at full-back and he scored twice, once direct from a corner at the Scoreboard end where I was standing. Really it did not matter so much who played well, only that United won the game – and with just about the whole ground and millions outside it willing them on, they beat Wednesday 3-0.

The message from chairman Harry Hardman on the front of that day's programme had started with the headline 'United Will Go On', and it seemed only right that they should set off on the long road back with a good win

As a footnote to the tragedy, only later did I realise that, if events a couple of years earlier had turned out differently, I too could have been on that plane in Munich. But that is another story and we'll come to it later.

The commemorative issue of the Manchester Evening News *twenty-five years after Munich.*

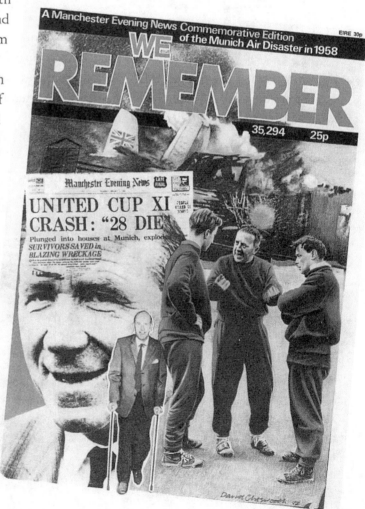

The emotional fifth-round Cup match against Sheffield Wednesday set United's recovery under way. Jimmy Murphy was still in charge as the makeshift team drove on in the Cup. They beat West Bromwich Albion in a quarter-final replay and then overcame Fulham 5-3 in a semi-final which also went to a second match.

Incredibly, after all that had happened, they had now reached the Final and were due to play Bolton Wanderers. Meanwhile in the League they had also hung on well; ninth place was the club's lowest since the war but in the circumstances it was very creditable.

The Cup Final was played on 3 May, just three months after Munich. Matt Busby was by then fit enough to travel to Wembley, and in the team they had four survivors from the crash – Bill Foulkes, Harry Gregg,

*The 1958 Cup Final. Matt Busby sits alongside Jimmy Murphy and **(below)** Dennis Viollet is stopped by the lunging tackle of a Bolton defender.*

UNITED THE LEGENDARY YEARS

Bobby Charlton and Dennis Viollet. Bolton, however, had Nat Lofthouse, the veteran England centre-forward, then aged 32 and determined to earn himself a Cup-winner's medal.

Fair enough, he put Bolton ahead in the third minute, but in the second half, while Harry Gregg was in the air going for a high ball, Lofthouse crashed into him and knocked him and the ball into the net. Hardly anybody could believe it when the referee pointed to the centre spot. Even allowing for the way the rules were applied in those days, you would have expected United to get a free-kick and Lofthouse, at the very least, a severe reprimand. Neither thing happened and that was the last of the scoring.

For Manchester United it was an unfortunate case of history repeating itself. The previous year, in the Cup Final against Aston Villa, their Peter McParland had charged quite unnecessarily into goalkeeper Ray Wood and smashed his cheekbone. It happened in the sixth minute and it cost United the Cup. Wood had to go off, Jackie Blanchflower took over in goal and United had to make the best of it with ten men as no substitutes were allowed at that time, not even for injured players. They lost 2-1 with, ironically, McParland scoring both Villa's goals just as Lofthouse was to do for Bolton the following year.

The next season, 1958-59, United did wonderfully well to finish runners-up in the League to Wolves. That alone says a lot for the partnership of Matt Busby and Jimmy Murphy. Matt, still not completely well but tactically as shrewd as ever, laying out the approach to each game and always interested in his players, making sure they felt OK, that their home lives were running smoothly, and encouraging them to give their best for United on the field.

Jimmy Murphy, on the other hand, was fiercer and more direct. He expected players to go for it 100 per cent, not just on match-days but on the training pitch as well. He hated shirkers or players who felt they had done enough and were then content just to coast the rest of the way.

It was Jimmy who gave a whole dynasty of United teams that essential fighting character which no successful side can do without. At the same time he urged on all his players, from the time they first joined the Youth team as young lads, how important it was to help everyone else in the side, to cover for them, to make yourself available, to get in there and battle when the game was tight, to keep going and never give up.

He was not above leading by example. Even in his fifties he loved to hurtle about the pitch in five-a-side games, taking the knocks as they came and always pushing the others on to do something faster or better.

That winter Matt Busby paid a British record transfer fee of £45,000 for inside forward Albert Quixall of Sheffield Wednesday. Quixall already had five England caps when he joined United at the age of 25, and Busby needed someone of experience and skill to influence the younger players. Jimmy Murphy's two emergency signings, Ernie Taylor and Stan Crowther, moved on to other clubs and Quixall settled down well in a partnership with Bobby Charlton that lasted six years.

Also in 1958-59 inside forward Dennis Viollet and winger Albert Scanlon, both injury victims in Munich, played a full part in the season. Out of a great total of 103 League goals, Bobby Charlton scored 29 and Scanlon 16. Bobby's total was one of United's highest ever, and the following season Dennis Viollet went three better with 32.

Even so, United were not the great team that Busby sought. To make matters worse, Wilf McGuinness broke his leg in an incident that more or less ended his career. It was still too soon for enough home-grown players to be coming through from the Youth and reserve teams, and to strengthen a leaky defence Busby brought in Maurice Setters from West Bromwich Albion and Noel Cantwell from West Ham. Setters, a mean-looking and tough-tackling wing-half, stayed with United for six years while Noel Cantwell, a long-standing Irish international, became a solid performer at left-back and rose to become club captain.

Di Stefano backheels the ball past Harry Gregg for Real Madrid's fourth goal in their 6-1 win over United in a specially arranged fixture in October 1959 which drew a crowd of 64,000.

LONDON MIDLAND

Shirts Red   MANCHESTER UNITED   Knickers White

GREGG

FOULKES
2
GREAVES
3

GOODWIN
4
COPE
8
McGUINNESS
6

WEBSTER
7
TAYLOR
8
DAWSON
9
CHARLTON
10
SCANLON
11

R   L

Referee:
J. C. Williams, Nottingham
Kick-off 3-0 pm
(Team changes indicated by loudspeaker)

FOOTBALL GREEN PLEASE

Linesmen:
A. Edge, Liverpool
Red Flag

K. Hiley, Burnley
Yellow Flag

L   R

ROBB
11
STOKES
10
SMITH
9
BROOKS
8
MEDWIN
7

ILEY
6
RYDEN
5
SHARPE
4

HOPKINS
3
BAKER
2

HOLLOWBREAD

TOTTENHAM HOTSPUR   Knickers Black

The 1958-59 line-up for the match against Tottenham which was to be Albert Quixall's first game for United; he replaced Ernie Taylor at No 8. Wilf McGuinness (left) was also in the team but he was to break his leg later in the season.. Another Quixall goal for United as he slots a penalty past Fulham goalkeeper Ken Hewkins at Craven Cottage in December 1960. Right An optimistic headline from the Evening Chronicle in 1962. Sadly Tottenham had the answer to the trump cards and won the semi-final.

UNITED FOR WEMBLEY!

MANCHESTER UNITED

This brilliant colour picture, taken by Evening Chronicle photographer Fred Armstrong, shows: Back row (left to right): Cantwell, Stiles, Charlton, Gaskell, Foulkes, Nicholson, Quixall. Front row: Lawton, Brennan, Herd, Setters, Dunne, Chisnall.

Charlton and Herd are the trump cards

By PETER SLINGSBY

SOCCER'S most glittering prize! That's how the FA Cup has long been regarded by clubs in this country, but in this season of sky-high wages and steadily falling "gates" it has taken on an even greater attraction.

A successful Cup run now provides a lifeline for many not-so-wealthy clubs. For the players, the Wembley trek is strewn with perks and much fatter pay packets because of match-by-match bonus increases and — for some — the extra cash based on attendance figures both at home and away.

Confident

Tottenham's stars have already netted a small fortune from their European Cup adventures — the club receipts topped £40,000 before the semi-finals—but at home the FA Cup competition is still the game's top moneyspinner.

Now Spurs are just one win away from repeating last year's visit to Wembley, where they made history by becoming the first team this century to pull off the magnificent double of Cup and League championship.

Barring Spurs' way are Manchester United, and there is confidence at Old Trafford that this is United's Cup year.

Nice blend

United have had some tremendous scraps to reach the club's fifth semi-final since the war. They knocked out fellow First Divisioners Bolton, Arsenal and Sheffield Wednesday—a formidable trio.

Then they had their closest call against Preston. an average Second Division side. Luck was undoubtedly with United in the quarter-final at Deepdale, but things went right in the replay.

Now, I'm solidly behind Maurice Setters and company in the view that they can get the better of silk-smooth Spurs at Hillsborough in a game which will climax a tremendous come-back by a club hard hit by injuries this season.

A well-ordered defence and a forward line nicely blended and capable of great football — that has been United's formula since the start of the Cup run, and they look to have the ideal make-up for a Wembley win.

This season they have taken three points from Spurs, and ace goal-poacher Jimmy Greaves has a healthy respect for a defence he has never mastered.

Ideal blend

In defence I rate United as having the edge over Spurs in skill and "bite." Spurs have already conceded eight Cup goals— twice as many as in their Cup run last season.

In attack Tottenham have struck a greater degree of consistency, but IN BUBBLING BOBBY CHARLTON AND DASHING DAVID HERD UNITED HAVE A COUPLE OF TRUMP CARDS, and the foraging of Nobby Lawton and the scheming of John Giles add up to a considerable threat to any defence in the country.

By two goals

Spurs will lay great store on Greaves's uncanny positional sense and finishing ability, and Cliff Jones and John White are additional threats to United's Wembley hopes.

But United's superb teamwork, that solid and surefooted defence, and an attack capable of extending the best in the world, let alone in this country, should see them through the semi-final.

Are Spurs—beaten 6—2 by Manchester City, over whom United have done the double—as good as they were last season? We shall soon know the answer.

IT LOOKS LIKE BEING A TIGHT GAME, BUT I'LL PLUMP FOR THE SCORE-LINE: MANCHESTER UNITED 2, TOTTENHAM 0.

Next on Busby's list of successful signings was David Herd, a Scottish international striker who came to Old Trafford from Arsenal at the age of 27, after Busby had been trying to sign him for two years.

Of all the players who came to the fore at United in the Sixties, maybe David Herd is the one who has received too little recognition. He had a phenomenal shot – which someone once timed at 72.5 mph – and scored 144 goals in the seven years he was at Old Trafford, before Brian Kidd came in and took over from him.

People may also forget that David was a great team player, and some of the goals he scored were big ones, including two against Leicester in the FA Cup Final of 1962-63 and 14 in European competitions, amongst them a hat-trick against ASK Vorwaerts of East Germany.

In a private way David was also an ideal United player. Matt Busby put a high value on family connections. He wanted to know how his new players were settling in and liked them to have a stable family relationship. In David's case he already knew the family well because he had played with David's father, Alec, at Manchester City.

At one time too, back in 1951, both the Herds had played together in the same team for Stockport County. So, in that sense, David was an excellent example of the player with a local background, someone who knew about life in Manchester and who also

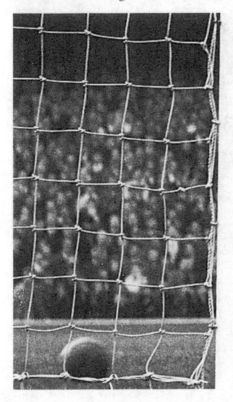

Right Tony Dunne dives in an attempt to stop a shot from Maurice Norman of Spurs at White Hart Lane in January 1962. Dave Mackay and Terry Dyson (No 11) watch as the ball lands on the top of the net. **Below** Another heavy defeat for United. George Eastham scores Arsenal's third goal in their 5-1 win at Highbury in October 1961.

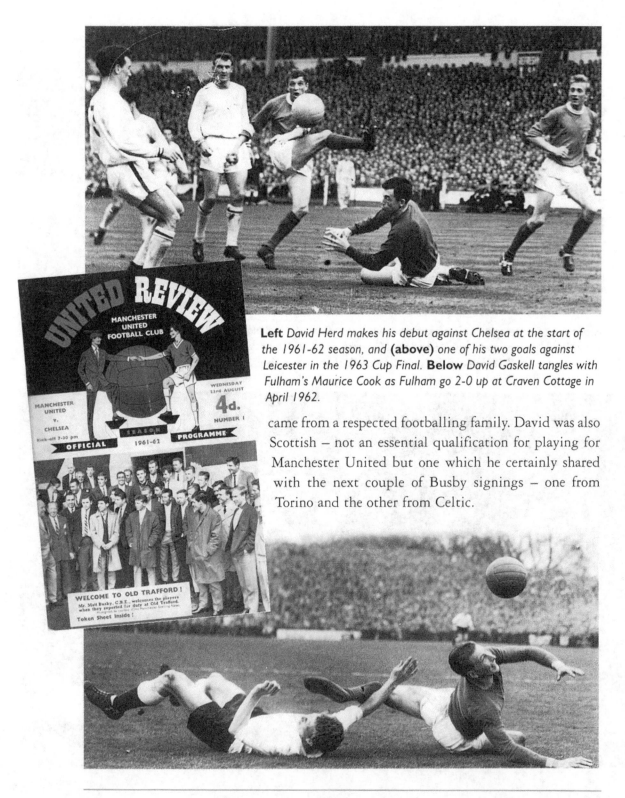

Left David Herd makes his debut against Chelsea at the start of the 1961-62 season, and **(above)** one of his two goals against Leicester in the 1963 Cup Final. **Below** David Gaskell tangles with Fulham's Maurice Cook as Fulham go 2-0 up at Craven Cottage in April 1962.

came from a respected footballing family. David was also Scottish – not an essential qualification for playing for Manchester United but one which he certainly shared with the next couple of Busby signings – one from Torino and the other from Celtic.

When Matt Busby began making inquiries about us, he was not exactly short of talented prospects. Already he had an unknown teenager from Ulster up his sleeve, by the name of George Best. He had signed him as a lad of 15, then had to fight to keep him when Bestie felt homesick and slipped off back to Belfast.

After that Busby let him develop quietly before he unleashed him on 14 September 1963 to the wider world, at the age of 17. In fact he fielded two 17 year-olds that day, the other being David Sadler who had joined the club as an amateur from Maidstone United in November 1962 and went on to be one of Manchester United's most durable players.

So while the manager had a number of promising young players on his books, he still thought he needed a couple more hardened professionals to round out the playing strength.

As for our own very different experiences of how we came to Old Trafford, let's take them in the order they took place.

Denis Law: *I was at Maine Road when I received this letter from the Sunday Dispatch in 1960. I was later presented with the plaque that went with the award.*

ASSOCIATED NEWSPAPERS, LTD
TELEPHONE: FLEET STREET 6000.
TELEGRAMS: SUNDAY DISPATCH, LONDON.

Sunday Dispatch

Editorial Department,
NORTHCLIFFE HOUSE,
LONDON. E.C. 4.

GR/MB

16th April, 1960.

Denis Law, Esq.,
Manchester City Football Club,
Maine Road,
Moss Side,
Manchester 14.

Dear Mr. Law,

I have pleasure in telling you that you have been chosen as inside left in the Great Britain Golden Boots XI. This team was selected by Andy Beattie, John Carey, Peter Doherty, Jimmy Murphy and George Swindin on behalf of the Sunday Dispatch to honour the Footballers of the Year.

We are awarding plaques to all the selected players and we should be honoured if you could attend the presentation ceremony at the Cornwall Room, Connaught Rooms, Great Queen Street, W.C.2. at 12 p.m. on April 27th.

Your manager Mr. L.J. McDowall has also been invited.

If you are able to attend we shall, of course, pay all your expenses.

Yours sincerely,

George Rutherford

George Rutherford
SPORTS EDITOR

R.S.V.P.

Denis Law: I had known Matt Busby for nearly four years before he signed me for United. And he, I found out later, had had his eyes on me for a couple of years before that. I had played for Huddersfield Town in a Youth Cup match against Manchester United. We played the game at Heckmondwike, just outside Huddersfield, on a pitch where, if you kicked the ball too hard over the touchline, it finished up in the canal.

It was not a great place for making an impression on anybody, but some time after the game Matt Busby put in an offer for me of £10,000. It never went any further because our manager, Andy Beattie, turned it down. That was an awful lot of money for a 16 year-old amateur who had barely started out in the game and had yet to make his League début. As it happened, I only heard about the offer much later, from Bill Shankly. It is also the reason why, as I mentioned earlier, I could have been on that plane at Munich.

In those days it was the normal thing for the manager of a national side to be a club manager at the same time. In October 1958 Matt Busby took charge of Scotland and picked me in his first team selection after I had made some forty League appearances in the Second Division for Huddersfield Town.

Denis Law: *The full compliment at Huddersfield. I am the player standing on the extreme right immediately behind the management. Can you recognise Bill Shankly seated second from the left in the row in front?*

It was a radical line-up with five Anglo-Scots in the forward line. Although the mixture set some Scottish heads wagging, it worked. We won 3-0 against Wales and I scored an 'accidental' goal when a clearance from their Dave Bowen cannoned off my head as I was walking back, and ballooned in past the goalkeeper, Jack Kelsey.

Matt kept picking me for Scotland and I became a team regular. The relationship continued after I had moved to Manchester City in March 1960 for a new British record fee of £55,000. At the time I had half-expected to follow my former manager, Bill Shankly, when he moved to Liverpool after three years in charge at Huddersfield (having taken over from Andy Beattie). It was Shanks in fact who had signed me up as a professional, the day after my 17th birthday. Later Shanks told me that he might have come in for me but Liverpool did not have the kind of money that he knew Huddersfield were bound to demand.

Denis Law: *My first transfer – signing for Manchester City in 1960 watched by City's manager Les McDowall.* **Right and below** *Postcard from Turin – Manchester City had played a friendly against Torino and I had stayed on, waiting for my transfer to the Italian club to be finalised.*

Similarly, Matt Busby had considered making a bid but then he held back. A few weeks after signing for City I ran into him by chance outside the Midland Hotel in Manchester.

'I would have come for you,' he told me, 'but our team is playing particularly well at the moment. Dennis Viollet is scoring a lot of goals and we've also got Albert Quixall, Alex Dawson and Bobby Charlton, so I didn't

Denis Law: *Enzo Bearzot was my captain at Torino and later went on to manage the Italian side that won the World Cup in 1982.* **Below** *Gerry Hitchens (centre), Joe Baker and I all played for the Italian League against the Football League at Old Trafford in November 1961.*

need to make an offer for you. But,' he added, 'you never know.'

I didn't stay long at City, who turned out to be a struggling side. I saw out two successful battles to avoid relegation but by June 1962 I was a Torino player, joining the growing wave of exiles who were going over to Italy. John Charles (Juventus) had been the first of the pioneers, and he and Eddie Firmani, who first went to Sampdoria and then moved on to other clubs, had made a great success of it. They paved the way for players like me, Jimmy Greaves (AC Milan), Gerry Hitchens (Inter Milan) and Joe Baker, who joined me at Torino from Hibernian.

Up till then footballers had not travelled much, and transfers were not as common as they are now. The maximum wage was only abolished in 1961 and before then players

Denis Law: *Souvenir of Italy, the Premio Limone was presented to me in 1961 by Tuttosport for being the most unco-operative player towards the press!*

could often see little point in going to a new and unknown club if they were still only going to earn the £20 a week they were already getting.

Italy was different. There the big clubs had money and were not afraid to flash it about, dangling the offer of high salaries and fat bonuses – £100 for a draw, £200 for a win – under the noses of young players, together with a signing-on fee in the region of £5000.

It was all very seductive. Of course, at the beginning they didn't tell you about the huge fines they used to impose on players, often for no reason at all, or about one or two other disadvantages it didn't take me long to come across, such as the fanatical press and the lunatic opposition supporters. At the time my only problem was one of choice – two Italian clubs were after me, Inter Milan and Torino.

Here what you might call the family-and-friends factor came into play. Football is full of chance encounters that can influence the future direction of a player's career. I think it will always be so, given the colleagues you meet at each club you play for, also the way each playing season goes round in a kind of cycle and you keep meeting up with people from other clubs who you know and like, and who may have something to say to you.

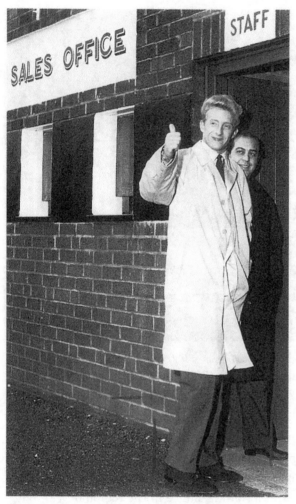

Denis Law: *This is it! Thumbs up to the press as I arrive at Old Trafford with Gigi Peronace of Torino to complete my transfer.*

The reason I signed for Torino had a lot to do with the fact that I had been playing with Joe Baker's brother Gerry at Manchester City, and had already met Joe a couple of times too. So the prospect of starting out in Italy in the company of another British player was what really swung it for me. Soon I was on a plane out to Turin.

I loved the city, the climate, the food and the wine. I preferred their training methods too – a combination of sprint and stamina training and ball skills, but with the emphasis much more on working with the ball. On match-days the man-to-man marking was hard to get used to, but at least I was able to roam about a bit – unlike Joe Baker who was a target man and spent most of his 90 minutes getting kicked by two markers who tracked him everywhere.

What really got me down in Italy was the negative football. Nobody wanted to play. Everybody sat back, week after week, grinding out results like 0-0, 1-1 and, very rarely, 2-0. It was this more than anything that made me determined to leave. And not only to leave, but to get back into football in England as quickly as possible. Other, less important turn-offs – though they all add up together in your mind – were the hostile away crowds, spitting at you from behind high wire fences like caged animals, run-ins with the press and long periods shut away in my apartment.

As early as the November, I mentioned my feelings to Matt Busby when we met after I had come over to play at Old Trafford for the Italian League against the Football League. I could not say much at the time, but six months later nothing at Torino had improved and I was in a stronger position to push for a transfer. I had another meeting with Matt Busby after a Scotland v England match at Hampden Park and he was able to reassure me that, if Torino were prepared to let me go, Manchester United would make an offer.

This duly went in, and the two clubs agreed a deal worth £115,000 – though not before the Torino officials had led Matt Busby on a ridiculous dance around Europe before he was able to pin them down at a meeting in Lausanne, Switzerland.

Then, to my amazement, Torino turned their back on the agreement with United and started trying to sell on my contract to their Turin rivals, Juventus, for a much more lucrative £160,000. In Italian law football clubs have a perfect right to sell on a player's contract to another club – and it may be that Torino had this in mind all along. So then we had this ridiculous position where I was being loaded with unwanted presents – a gold watch and a gold tie-pin – and promised a signing-on fee of £12,000 if I agreed to do what they wanted and join Juventus.

I was having none of it. So far as I was concerned, I was about to become a Manchester United player and that was the end of it. I left Turin for the last time and flew back to Scotland. Torino were furious and threatened to ban me from playing in any country registered with FIFA. It was a nerve-wracking time but I sat it out. If I had lost my case and been banned, the most likely playing options were a new career in South Africa or Australia, which were not then affiliated to FIFA. I did not fancy any of them – what player would, if he knew Manchester United wanted to sign him?

Denis Law: *I have done my bit and now Les Olive, the club's secretary, completes the paperwork for Manchester United, watched by Gigi Peronace, Matt Busby and Jimmy Murphy.*

retain the player may be refused. Professional players so retained remain the registered players of the Clubs, unless and until they satisfy the Council that there are special grounds for allowing them to change their Clubs. Clubs must at once report to this Association that they have given notice to the player, and also inform the player they have done so. A Club desirous of withdrawing the retainer must at once give notice to the Association, and a player shall not be registered until notice has been received. A League or Combination of Clubs, other than the Football League, may, by its Rules, and for its own Competition, make provision for the retention of professional players by its Clubs to whom the Clubs are prepared to pay at the rate of two pounds for each week during the period of the playing season. Players so retained shall have a right of appeal to the Association which sanctioned the Competition. A player under suspension may be re-signed by his Club subject to the terms of his suspension. (c) Payment to Agents. No payment shall be made to agents or other persons than Clubs and players concerned in the engagement of players except to persons in the Club's regular employment.

Rule 29. (a) Clubs must have written agreements with their professional players stating all the terms of the engagements, and such agreements must be completed when the player signs the registration form. (b) Cancellation of Agreement. Agreements may provide that a professional player shall only be paid when played in matches but if any such player is not played for a period of four weeks, he may apply to the Club to cancel his agreement and registration, and if refused he shall be at liberty to apply to this Association for the cancellation of the agreement upon such terms as may be deemed reasonable. Where conditions, other than payment of wages for playing football form part of an agreement, this Association in dealing with claims thereunder will restrict its investigations and decisions solely to the question of wages for playing as stipulated in the agreement. Except by mutual consent a Club or Player shall not be entitled to determine the agreement between them without the consent of the Council of this Association in accordance with Rule 30. When an agreement has been determined by mutual consent, notice signed by the Club and the player shall at once be sent to the Association who will cancel the registration. (c) Disciplinary Suspension. A Club not desirous of putting into force the larger powers contained in Rule 30 shall, in the case of misconduct by a player, or breach of the training or disciplinary rules or orders of the Club have the right to suspend such player for a period not exceeding fourteen days or impose a fine not exceeding two weeks' wages; but the Club shall notify this Association of such suspension or fine within two days and the player may, on lodging a deposit fee of £1, appeal to this Association against such action by the Club. The suspension or fine shall not operate as a termination or cancellation of the agreement between the Club and the player.

Name of Player (in full) _Denis Law_

Present Postal Address _23, Goulden Road, Withington, Manchester_

Club for which Player last played _A.C. Torino_

Place of Birth _Aberdeen_   Date of Birth _24. 2. 40_
                                             (CONFIDENTIAL—FOR RECORD PURPOSES ONLY)

I hereby consent to be registered as a Professional Player by the

Manchester United Football Club (* _Lancashire_ Association)
                                   *Insert name of County Association to which the Club belongs

from .... to .... and I undertake to

observe the Rules, Regulations, and Bye-Laws of The Football Association.

Signed by the said Player in the presence of

Signature of Witness } ....

Address of Witness } ....

Signature of Player } _Denis Law_

Date _12th July_ 19_62_

TO THE SECRETARY OF THE FOOTBALL ASSOCIATION, 22 Lancaster Gate, London, W.2.

On behalf of the .... Football Club,

I request you to register .... as a Professional Player.

L. Olive .... Secretary.

Date .... 19 .... Address.

Half-a-crown is charged for each form. All forms must be sent to the Secretary, The Football Association, at 22 Lancaster Gate, London, W.2. accompanied by a copy of the Agreement entered into between the Club and the Player.

SEASON .... **FORM G (2)**

No. G/2 . 33807   THE FOOTBALL ASSOCIATION
                   REGISTRATION OF A PROFESSIONAL PLAYER

I hereby certify that I have this day registered ....

as a Professional Player for .... Club

Date .... { Secretary of
                                                                  { The Football Association

Denis Law: *At last I am officially registered as a Manchester United player on 12 July 1962. Expectation was high in the press but I was already concerned about my knee. I had already had a cartilage operation and it was to be a recurring problem throughout my career.*

LAW? HE COULD TOP PELE

—says Murphy

By DON HARDISTY

"DENIS LAW could be even better than Pele." That opinion came yesterday from one well qualified to judge—Manchester United assistant manager Jimmy Murphy, who has managed the Welsh team three times in four years against the might of Brazil and the artistry of their little supremo.

Matt Busby nodded his agreement as the pair of them watched Law, in a startling shirt of many colours go through his first training session with his new club-mates.

Summary of the debate which followed: While Pele was a master footballer in one half of the field, Law was the complete inside forward because he spread his talents over both halves.

Added Busby: "I think he can help everybody in the side to cut out the aimless stuff which crept into our play last season."

26th November, 1962.

Dear Dr. McHugh,

      re: Denis Law.

        I saw this player yesterday at the Club. You will remember that we saw him together on Saturday during the match, when he sustained a forced abduction strain of the right knee joint.

        There was some tenderness over the medial ligament at its middle and slight laxity, but I think that this is due to the old cartilage lesion and the fact that he has had his external cartilage removed previously, rather than to the present injury.

        I think that this is a ligamentous strain and I am happy to say that the prognosis is good and that it will not interfere with his future as a player.

        As we discussed with Mr. Dalton, he is to have quadriceps exercises and faradism daily.

        Kind regards,

            Yours sincerely,

Dr. McHugh,
c/o The Manchester United
     Football Club,
Trafford Park,
MANCHESTER, 16.

For about two months I kept my head down in Aberdeen, banking on the idea that Torino would not be prepared to sacrifice the £115,000 which was in the bag just for the pleasure of seeing me banned from playing where I wanted to. In the end it worked out my way. Torino gave in and I signed for Manchester United on 12 July 1962.

It was my third move in two years and each time the fee had broken the British record. For me the money was not the important thing. What I wanted most of all was a club where I could at last settle down and play good football.

Pat Crerand: The team I supported as a kid in Scotland was Celtic. I knew about Manchester United even in those days because of the great players they had. And everybody knew about Matt Busby because he had wanted to play for Celtic at one time and he came from a place not far from Glasgow.

As well as that there has always been a good relationship between Celtic and Manchester United. Jimmy Delaney was a great Scottish winger from the 1940s and he went down to Manchester from Celtic in 1946 — he was one of Matt Busby's first signings and he was in the side which won the FA Cup in 1948. In more recent times Lou Macari and Brian McClair also came down from Celtic to play for United, so it has been quite a steady connection.

In 1962 I had been at Celtic for five years and had been picked several times for Scotland, which is how I first got to know Denis. Then a time came when the club was not doing very well and I was not happy about the way they were playing. To me there was too much kick-and-rush about it. All the same the prospect of leaving had not really come into it, or at least nothing had been firmly said on either side.

When it came about, it was like a bolt from the blue — which tells you something about how players were treated in those days.

Denis has explained how he could have got banned for life from playing in Britain or Europe because his Italian club had special rights over what he did and where he went. In my case it was quite incredible what happened.

I was courting at the time, and we were at the seven o'clock Mass on a Sunday evening at St Francis's Church in Glasgow. I came back after the Mass to my mother's house and there was a little guy there, Jim Rodgers, who worked for the *Daily Express*.

He said, 'You're going to Manchester United.'

I was just totally amazed. Nobody had asked me what I thought. As far as the management was concerned it was never a case of 'Do you want to go to Manchester

Pat Crerand: *This is me in my early days at Parkhead. Willie Fernie, who later went to Middlesbrough, watches me showing off my ball skills. Note the impressive training kit we Celtic players wore in those days!*

United?' – just 'You're going.' And I had to get the information about it from a newspaper man.

'Yes,' he said. 'Matt Busby's been up. He's done the deal with Bob Kelly. You're going.'

Looking back it seems dreadful by today's standards, but in those days it was what happened. A player had to change his whole life, his whole culture just because his employers at the football club could do what they wanted. And there was nothing the player could do about it.

Afterwards I found out a bit more about the background to it. About how Denis, for one, had been involved in recommending me. Apparently, Matt Busby had been interested in me and Jimmy Baxter of Rangers, and he had asked Denis which player he thought would be best for United. Denis had told him he thought Baxter was a more skilful player, but if he was looking for the one who would be the better long-term investment for Manchester United, then he ought to go for me.

Matt always spoke to players about players. If you want a good opinion about a player you ask somebody who has played against him a few times. That can give you a good idea of what the player's all about and what he could do for your team.

So there it was. I wasn't a Celtic player any more, I was a Manchester United player. I travelled to Manchester on 5 February 1963 and signed the forms the next day. Going down there gave me the biggest cultural shock of my life.

Pat Crerand: *Two memories of the final months before my arrival at Old Trafford. The dressing-room passes for the international against Wales and my last 'old-firm' game at Ibrox.*

THE RANGERS FOOTBALL CLUB

IBROX STADIUM
GLASGOW, S.W.3

THE RANGERS
FOOTBALL CLUB

1 JAN 1963

Available for this date only

PLAYER'S
Admission Ticket

ENTER BY
MAIN ENTRANCE
EDMISTON DRIVE

THE FOOTBALL ASSOCIATION OF WALES
LIMITED

Admit to Dressing Room

PLAYERS' ENTRANCE

WALES
V.
SCOTLAND
NINIAN PARK
CARDIFF
SATURDAY,
20th OCTOBER, 1962

Secretary.

A FAMILY TYPE OF PLACE

Pat Crerand: My first impressions of Manchester were quite something. All those red-brick buildings! I had lived my whole life in Glasgow and there most of the place is built in a warm reddish-yellow stone, which then would be quickly covered in soot, so the feel of everything I looked at was completely different.

It was also, in many ways, a bigger, more bustling kind of place, inhabited by many more different races. We had a few Pakistanis in Glasgow but I had never seen so many West Indians on the streets as I found in Manchester. I am not a racist in any way whatever but it was a totally strange environment.

And digs! I had to stay in digs. I was 22 at the time and I had never stayed anywhere before except in my mother's house. Here I was lucky. The club put me in touch with Mrs Scott, who was a lovely woman and looked after me really well. I had beautiful digs, like a self-contained apartment, and that was maybe the easiest part of moving down to Manchester.

Pat Crerand: *I brought Noreen with me to get a first sight of Manchester when I arrived to sign for United.*

There was another important cultural thing, and that had to do with my family background, and also my fiancée's. We were engaged when we first came down to Manchester, and we both of us found it a very strange place.

She had never been away from home either. Both her parents and mine were Irish and the only time we ever went out of town from Glasgow was to go to Ireland. England was a totally foreign land. Her father was very very Irish, which means that he was not particularly pro-England, so in his eyes Manchester was not the best of places for his daughter to go – some terrible kind of pagan land.

He got used to it in the end. In fact he loved it whenever he came down to see us, but in the early days he certainly had his doubts. You have also to think that both our

Pat Crerand: *Noreen and I got married in Glasgow soon after the end of my first season at Old Trafford. Denis and Di had been married in Aberdeen the previous December.*

parents were fervent Celtic supporters, so when I decided to leave the club – their club – that too was a shock to the system.

And not just Manchester, but the club itself was different. It was obviously a big club, a lot bigger than Celtic. And here I was, going into a totally new place – I had never been to Old Trafford before in my life – and meeting a squad of about forty players for the first time.

Denis was the only one I knew at all well, because we had played together for Scotland. I had also met Noel Cantwell, but I don't think I knew the others at all.

This was where Matt Busby showed what a good manager he was. I had never spoken to him before the transfer deal was arranged. Then I flew down to Manchester to meet him and visit the club.

I arrived at Manchester Airport with my fiancée and there was Matt Busby to meet us, together with Louis Edwards who was to become the club chairman two years later. Matt had also brought along Denis and Di, his wife, who we had met before up in Scotland.

That was my first introduction to Manchester and it did a lot to reassure me. Next day I signed the forms and that was me committed to my new club.

Denis Law: I did not have the same problems as Pat, because I had travelled about more and played for other big clubs. Also I had played at City for just over a year, so I knew something about Manchester and went straight back into the same digs I had lived in when I was at City. My host family were Mr and Mrs Atkins, and they looked after me like one of their own until I got married in December 1962.

The only thing I did not know about was how to get to Old Trafford from my digs. The first time I was to due to go in, I had to ask someone the way. All my previous journeys to and from the Atkins's house had been made with Maine Road in mind, and I did not have a clue about United's ground.

What's more, I shared these digs with a City player, Sandy Wann. For anyone steeped in the legends of local rivalry and big-city derby matches, the arrangements in our house would have seemed a little strange. Every morning Sandy went off to train with City and I went off to Old Trafford.

The real difference for me was on the pitch. After a year of being marked man-to-man in Italy, where the trick was to go roaming and try to shake off the marker, I found that I had put on a yard of pace and also that I was not being marked nearly as tightly. With all this extra time and space I could lose players more easily and score goals, which was obviously what United had bought me for.

The important thing about Manchester United was that the players were looked after extremely well. You had the feeling you could not have been better off anywhere else. This was all Matt Busby's doing. He wanted players to feel special from the moment he signed them.

Before that he would have done a lot of homework on the player, and by the time he was close to making an offer he would know a great deal about someone's playing ability. There was something else as well. He wanted to know what kind of person the player was, how he lived and whether he behaved himself or not.

He wanted people with a stable background. He liked them to be married and to have a family. If they had these responsibilities they would be less likely to go out nightclubbing or be off to bars. He wanted to create a family atmosphere in the club and for this to communicate itself to all the players and their families. He even asked about your parents, and with his younger players he took a lot of care to meet them and make sure the boy had the kind of digs where he would be as happy as possible, and that the parents knew the host family and exactly what kind of a set-up it was.

At United under Busby you were never just a player who performed on match-days.

Denis Law: *Family life away from Old Trafford: practising my golf swing in the garden; doing my bit in the kitchen; on holiday with son Gary at Llandudno: teaching Gary the basics.*

We played quite a bit of golf in our spare time. On this occasion it was a three-ball with Maurice Setters while we were at Blackpool preparing for a cup-tie in 1963.

You were an individual with a family to look after. He would always be asking about your wife and kids, and your mother and father and your brothers and sisters. He wanted to know if you were all right and content in your home life. If you were happy off the pitch, then it would be a lot easier for you to go out on match-days and play to the best of your ability.

He also involved the players in his own family's activities. There were lots of parties, and christenings as well. He had seven grandchildren at the time, or thereabouts, so there were plenty of christenings.

It was quite funny. Christenings were always on a Sunday, which was our day off. But we might be playing again on the Wednesday, so at eleven o'clock – Out! – we were slung. There was training the next day and we had to look after ourselves and be fit to play. The wives could stay on, but Matt Busby would look at the players in no uncertain terms and that would be, 'You. Up!' And off we had to go, leaving our wives to finish the party along with all the Busbys.

United were already known as a great family club before we joined. It was something Matt had been doing ever since he took over at the end of the war, and it was the basis on which he had built his great side of the Forties and the Busby Babes after that.

On the field it meant that you were always prepared to battle for each other, and also, because of the style of football he had established at the club, you were always encouraged to play, to show what you could do.

Ever since the 1940s, all Busby's teams played the same style of attractive football, and this went right through the club. They all played the same way, from the first team down to the reserves and the Youth side. It gave the whole club a continuity on the pitch and it made it easier to draft in new players to fit a particular role. It would then be up to the new player to make something of it.

John Fitzpatrick (centre) and Francis Burns board the team bus with trainer Jack Crompton and goalkeeper Jimmy Rimmer, another product of the youth team.

Just because you were in the Youth team or the reserves did not mean you were in any way inferior. Everybody was treated exactly the same and age did not count for anything. If you were good enough, you were good enough. Matt was always looking to encourage new young players.

All through the Sixties we had new home-grown players coming into the side. It was never just for the sake of change, but every year in football a team has to make some adjustments. Established players will lose their edge or get an injury – and with the massive fixture lists we were building up with the League, FA Cup and regular long runs in Europe, we were always needing new people.

By 1968 we had Brian Kidd come into the side and after that he was never out of it. Frannie Burns played in nearly every European Cup game except the semi-final and the Final. They were lads who had played together in the Youth team. Others were John Aston and John Fitzpatrick.

If the Youth team had a match, it was usual for five or six first-team players to go down there and watch them. You wanted to see the young players coming through, and they were always exciting games anyway.

When you look at the team that played in the European Cup Final in 1968, there were only two bought-in players, Pat Crerand and Alex Stepney (Denis unfortunately was injured and did not play). All the rest had come up through the club. Without the family atmosphere to keep everyone together, that might never have happened.

Pat Crerand: *Matt Busby was a good friend for so many years. This is a letter he wrote for me in 1981.*
Left *Photocall with Noreen and the family after I had been selected for Scotland against England at Wembley in 1965.*

210 KINGS ROAD

CHORLTON

MANCHESTER 21

14th September 1981

Dear Sir,

To Whom it may Concern.

I have known Pat. Crerand for around twenty years, having signed him as a player for Manchester United F.C., while I was Manager of the Club.

I have found him at all times a man of splendid Character, Trestworthy with a very happy personality.

So I am very happy indeed, to recommend him for any position, he wishes to undertake.

I Remain
Yours Truly,
M. Busby

Denis Law: My début was very important to me. The club had spent a lot of money to bring me over from Italy – something like double the going rate for a British player – and I naturally felt a big obligation to them when I first stepped out at Old Trafford.

It was a full house – which meant more than 50,000 spectators – and we were playing West Bromwich Albion.

I got off to a magnificent start. Within ten minutes

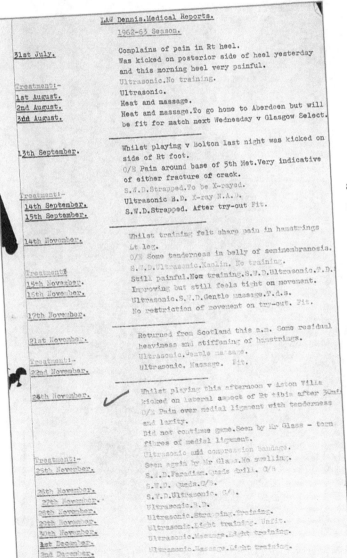

a cross came over and I connected with a header from about ten yards – which was a long way for me – and that was my first goal for United.

We went into a two-goal lead, which was great for my début, but unfortunately by the end of the 90 minutes West Bromwich had managed to pull back a couple of goals. It was still a good start, but I'd love to have won it.

Denis Law: *United kept a medical log for all players and this was mine for my first season at Old Trafford - the usual knocks but nothing too serious.*

Denis Law: *The photographers were at my first training session with United. This serious training exercise involves myself and Maurice Setters against Albert Quixall and Shay Brennan.*

Pat Crerand: My début came later that season after the bad winter had set in. The weather was so bad, we could not get a game in England for weeks, so Manchester United fixed up a couple of friendlies in Ireland, where for some reason they did not have so much ice and snow, especially by the coast.

I made my début for United in Cork, of all places. We played Bolton Wanderers and beat them 4-2, and I scored in that game. It was a vicious goal. The ball came to

Pat Crerand: *Early days in United colours.*

me just outside the 18-yard line. It was a new pitch – I don't think it had ever been played on before – and it was lashing with rain. So I hit this left-footed drive. Ferocious it was, with so much power. It flew through the air like some deadly balloon, and in their goal Eddie Hopkinson stood waiting for it. It took ages to reach him but, just as he was bending down to pick it up, it must have hit a brick or something and it went off past him into the opposite side of the goal.

Sponsored by Cork   Schoolboys' League

ASSOCIATION FOOTBALL

Exhibition Match . . .

Manchester United

v.

Bolton Wanderers

FLOWER LODGE - - CORK

Wednesday - 13th February - 196

Programme Price Sixpence   No   71

It was one of the finest goals I ever struck – not that there were all that many – and it happened on my début for United.

Pat Crerand: *There are not too many of these programmes about. This is one I signed for friend and collector Ray Adler.*

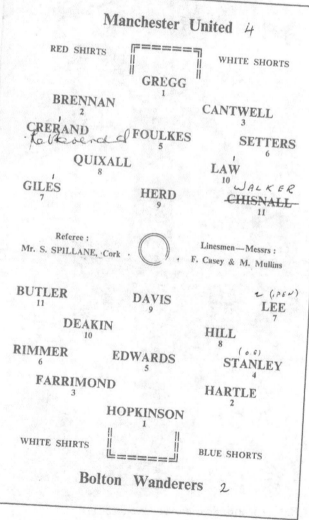

Manchester United *4*

RED SHIRTS   WHITE SHORTS

GREGG
1

BRENNAN   CANTWELL
2   3

CRERAND   FOULKES   SETTERS
5   6

QUIXALL   LAW
8   10

GILES   HERD   *WALKER*
7   9   ~~CHISNALL~~
11

Referee :
Mr. S. SPILLANE, .Cork ·   Linesmen—Messrs :
F. Casey & M. Mullins

BUTLER   DAVIS   *(PEN)*
11   9   LEE
7

DEAKIN
10   HILL
8

RIMMER   EDWARDS   *(o.g)*
6   5   STANLEY
4

FARRIMOND   HARTLE
3   2

HOPKINSON
1

WHITE SHIRTS   BLUE SHORTS

Bolton Wanderers *2*

For all its earlier post-war successes, the club was struggling when we joined. There was no more money around to buy new players and United were slipping and sliding in the League. In 1961-62, without our help, they had finished 15th, and in our first playing season it looked for a long time as if we might be relegated.

It was five years after Munich, and since then Matt Busby had been steadily rebuilding his side but without ever reaching the heights of the pre-Munich team. In their first year after the crash they did extremely well. As we have seen, they got to the Cup Final three months afterwards, and next season they finished second in the League.

All the same, it looks now as if they somehow survived that first year on emotion – the will to fight, which they themselves felt, and the amazing support they received from the public. Even in

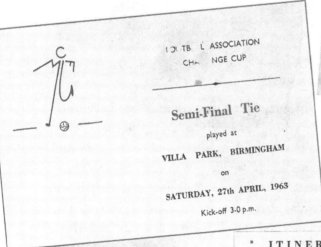

This time the Evening Chronicle's optimistic headline was to be proved correct, and we went on to beat Southampton 1-0 at Villa Park. The itinerary below gave us our orders for the day.

FOOTBALL ASSOCIATION CHALLENGE CUP

Semi-Final Tie

played at

VILLA PARK, BIRMINGHAM

on

SATURDAY, 27th APRIL, 1963

Kick-off 3-0 p.m.

" ITINERARY "

OFFICIAL TRAVELLING PARTY

Time	Event	Time	Event
8-30 a.m.	Depart Old Trafford	5-00 p.m.	Depart from Ground
10-15 a.m.	Coffee at Crown Hotel, Stone	6-30 p.m.	Tea and Sandwiches at Crown Hotel, Stone
10-45 a.m.	Depart	7-00 p.m.	Depart
12-00 p.m.	Arrive Queens Hotel, Birmingham	8-30 p.m.	Approximate time of arrival in Manchester
12-15 p.m.	Lunch	9-00 p.m.	Dinner and Dance, Midland Hotel
2-00 p.m.	Depart for Ground	1-00 a.m.	Carriages
3-00 p.m.	Kick-off		

Shay Brennan covers on the goal-line as Tony Dunne and Harry Gregg deal with a Coventry attack in the 1963 Cup quarter-final at Highfield Road which we won 3-1.

the opposition teams there was maybe a feeling that they would rather not have to be playing against Manchester United after everything that had happened to them.

The 1962-63 season began quite well, but then that hard winter set in around Boxing Day and matches were being postponed and postponed. We didn't play a League game for about ten weeks. When the weather cleared up, we had not even started our run in the Cup so we had an enormous backlog of matches that had to be played. The season had to be extended, which was very rare, and the Cup Final was put back three weeks until the end of May.

It was the same for other clubs with Cup commitments, but at United we somehow got into a rut of not scoring enough goals and letting too many in at the back.

In the relegation battle we went close to the wire. With four matches to go it was certain only that Leyton Orient would be relegated. Two teams went down in those days, and the other clubs in the drop zone were Birmingham City and the two Manchester Clubs, City and United.

We went to Birmingham for our next match and lost 2-1. Our next game was against City at Maine Road. By then they were in an even more desperate state than we were and really needed both points, whereas we knew that a draw would be enough — provided we also won our last home game against Leyton Orient. Denis can tell the story of what happened next.

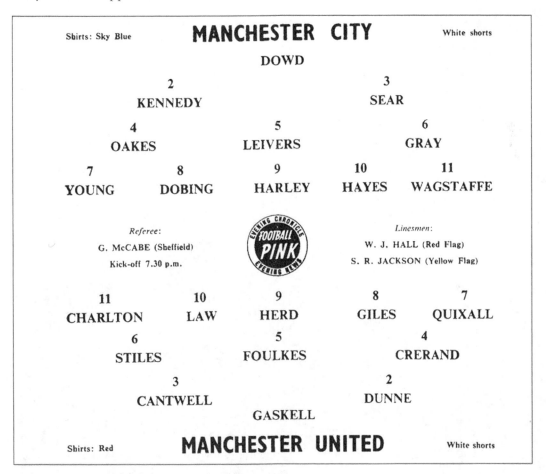

The teams as they lined up for the vital relegation battle at Maine Road.

Denis Law: City took an early lead through Alex Harley and they held on well after that. In the second half it was still 1-0 to them and I was in the penalty area with the ball. I was going nowhere, out towards the edge of the box when Harry Dowd, their goalkeeper, came after me and pulled me down with a kind of rugby tackle.

There was no question about the penalty decision. Albert Quixall took it, I looked the other way, and the ball ended up in the net. We took the point back home with us and next week beat the Orient 3-1. We were safe, and City were relegated.

Seven days later we were at Wembley for the Cup Final, against Leicester. They had come close to winning the League and were hot favourites. We were happy to be the underdogs because, especially at Wembley, there is a tendency to freeze up if you feel too much is expected of you. We had none of that and were

Denis Law: *We were in relaxed mood at the Cup Final headquarters in Weybridge, but I can't remember why I should be carrying the shoeless Maurice Setters across the car park.*

Pat Crerand: *After David Herd and Bill Foulkes, Noel Cantwell presents Denis and myself to the Duke of Edinburgh before the Cup Final, Tony Dunne waits in line.*

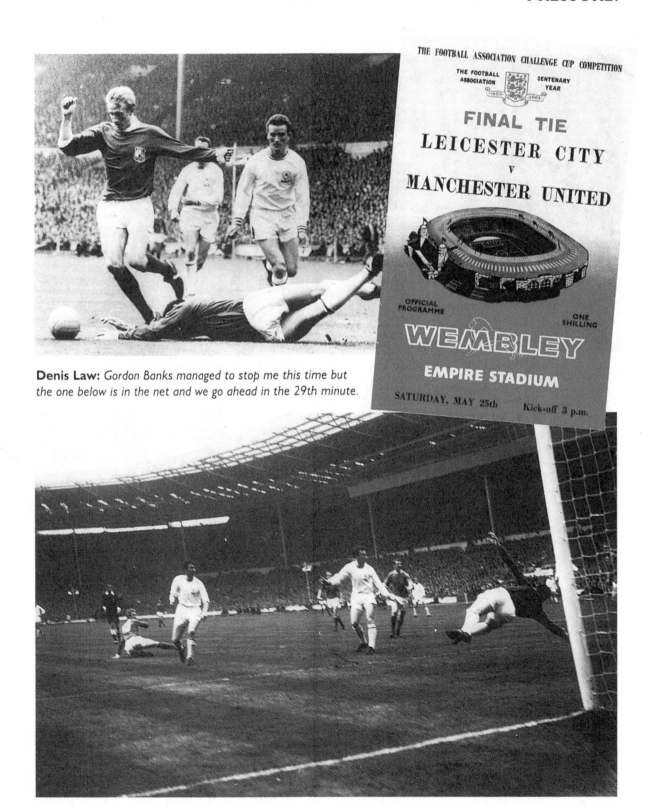

Denis Law: *Gordon Banks managed to stop me this time but the one below is in the net and we go ahead in the 29th minute.*

THE FOOTBALL ASSOCIATION CHALLENGE CUP COMPETITION

THE FOOTBALL ASSOCIATION · CENTENARY YEAR · 1863-1963

FINAL TIE
LEICESTER CITY
v
MANCHESTER UNITED

OFFICIAL PROGRAMME — ONE SHILLING

WEMBLEY
EMPIRE STADIUM

SATURDAY, MAY 25th   Kick-off 3 p.m.

Pat Crerand: *Only a few weeks at United and I am already collecting a Cup-winner's medal from the Queen.* **Below** *Matt Busby's first trophy since the tragedy of Munich.*

able to play our natural attacking game. Our team that day was: Gaskell; Dunne, Cantwell (captain); Crerand, Foulkes, Setters; Giles, Quixall, Herd, Law, Charlton.

This was more or less the side which would see us into the beginning of our great period in the mid-1960s. So far, though, we had not proved ourselves at all.

Denis Law: *Noel Cantwell, the captain, keeps hold of the Cup as we do the traditional lap of honour around Wembley.* **Left** *Maurice Setters and David Herd grab the handles and I get crowned with the lid – while Bobby Charlton relaxes with a cigarette. How times have changed!*

Wembley is a big pitch and a kind place to teams who have the ability to stroke the ball about and play a bit. We felt we could do that. We had the skills of Albert Quixall, then we had Bobby and Pat to push the ball through, and, in Bobby and David Herd, two of the fiercest strikers of the ball in British football. At the back we had our hard men, especially Bill Foulkes, Maurice Setters and Noel Cantwell, and we needed them to be at their best because Leicester were also an adventurous, mobile team.

Red and white on the menu for the banquet at The Savoy after our Cup Final success, and win or lose we already had invitations to a Lord Mayor's reception at the Town Hall the following day.

We took the lead in the 29th minute when Denis scored from a through pass by Pat. After that we dominated the game. David Herd added two more and we ran out 3-1 winners. It was probably our best game of the season. We really clicked for the first time, and we could have won it by six goals.

Every side needs something to help them on their way. For us this Cup Final was our turning-point. We had showed what we could do, and from then on we knew there was little or nothing in the game that we could not achieve.

Pat Crerand: One personal memory of that Cup Final. I had never seen a Cup Final at Wembley, not even on television.

We stayed at Oatlands Park in Weybridge. I woke up about half-past ten and after that it was a laugh and a giggle all the way – not a sign of nerves from anybody.

We arrived at Wembley and I got changed. I didn't put my top on because it was a warm summer's day – the Cup Final was played on 27 May that year. Then I went out of the dressing-room. I could hear the crowd singing 'Abide With Me' so I went down to the end of the tunnel and had a look round at it all. I thought it was completely fantastic – the singing and the whole occasion, that old guy in his red-white-and-blue England supporters' suit, everybody waving their programmes and looking forward to the big game.

I must have stood down there for five or six minutes, watching it all. When I got back to the dressing room, Matt Busby was going potty: 'Where's Crerand?' So I'm sorry if I caused him a bit of anxiety but it was worth it to me just to see what a special occasion Wembley is. As for the game itself, Denis has told me that although he scored a goal – in fact he clearly remembers it going in past Gordon Banks – after that he can't remember a thing about the game. I know how he feels. A Cup Final game at Wembley is every player's dream, but when you're out there playing, the time goes by so fast it's over before you've had a chance to think about it.

Winning the Cup in 1963 was the start of five years of success for United. It did not come immediately, it seldom does, and the next season was, in the light of what we achieved later, a relative failure.

We came second in the League which was, admittedly, a big improvement on the previous year when we finished 19th and almost went down. In the FA Cup we reached the semi-final but then we were knocked out by West Ham. We were also in Europe, in the Cup Winners' Cup. Even in those days, English clubs were suffering from a massive fixture congestion. At the end of the season everything was so condensed, in the space of three weeks we had to play three sixth-round FA Cup matches against Sunderland, two European Cup Winners' Cup quarter-finals, an important League match and an FA Cup semi-final.

There was no allowance made for the players. The FA made us play all those matches one on top of the other, and so you never got any rest. It was not so much the rest physically, it was the lack of mental rest that counted against you.

In one particular week it all went wrong for us. We had been drained by the three Cup games against Sunderland, and by the time of the semi-final we were very tired.

Pat Crerand: I remember the semi-final against West Ham particularly well because we played at Sheffield Wednesday on a pitch that was horrendous.

I went out to look at the pitch before the game. I was standing where the players come out, the rain was hammering down and the referee came out. He threw the ball down to test the bounce and it stuck flat in the mud and didn't come up again.

Denis Law: *A goal against Sporting Lisbon at Old Trafford but we were dumped out of the Cup Winners' Cup in the return match.*

to win something. He had been so close before with his wonderful 1950s team, and not to do better this time must have been very hard.

One very important introduction to the side in that season was the début of George Best. After we won the Cup the previous season Johnny Giles was sold to Leeds United and that created a vacancy out on the wing.

At first we thought George looked too frail for the rigours of the First Division. He was very skinny for a footballer and we wondered if he had the stamina to survive. He showed us all very quickly that he could look after himself. He had terrific speed, he rode the tackles and got his own in without shirking. He was a natural two-footed player with a great shot and he was a good header too. If we ever had a criticism of him on the field, it was that he sometimes held on to the ball too long when he might have done better to pass it.

George was a great player for all that, one of the finest. In his first season he scored some wonderful goals and his career was already well set for the future. After 15 matches with us he was picked for Northern Ireland. Although they were not a strong side he always put on something special for them, ending up with 37 international caps.

Pat Crerand: I remember seeing George play in a Youth team match at Old Trafford not long after I came to the club. I couldn't believe how good he was so I had a word with Jack Crompton, their coach.

'Oh, yes,' he said. 'We know all about him. We're just keeping him under wraps until he's a little bit older.'

Nobby Stiles played his first game for the club in 1960.

Bestie gave United that extra cutting edge at the front that Johnny Giles had not quite been able to provide. Johnny had played well for United but it was not until Don Revie developed a midfield role for him that he showed his true abilities. Strangely, this was something he had shown no sign of wanting to do while he was with us.

Also in the 1963-64 season we got our defence working better. The new partnership of Crerand and Stiles gave us Pat's creative ability allied to Nobby's dedicated knack of stopping people.

Surely it would not be long before we won something really big.

Denis Law: *After the excitement of winning my first Cup Final at Wembley I was back there again a month later for a match to celebrate the Centenary of the Football Association. I was chosen to play in a Rest of the World XI against England. Jim Baxter **(right)**, my Scottish team-mate, was also in the side. The full line-up **(above)** was: Back row (left to right): Ferenc Puskas, Djalma Santos, Svatopluk Pluskal, Lev Yashin, Jan Popluhar, Karl Heinz Schnellinger, Milutin Soskic, Josef Masopust, Luis Eyzaguirre, Uwe Seeler (Jim Baxter was also there but is hidden behind Seeler). Front row: Raymond Kopa, myself, Alfredo di Stefano, Ferreira da Silva Eusebio, Francisco Gento. I scored the only goal for the Rest of the World but we went down 2-1.*

Manchester United were a great club in the Sixties, by anybody's standards, but the facilities were not a patch on what they had at the big European clubs.

In Italy, for example, football was all, and still is today. It's all they have, that is their life. There is no other sport to match it. And the clubs looked after their players and gave them everything. After all, the players are any club's principal asset, and without them no club would get anywhere. So they gave them proper boots or shoes, whatever you called them. All the kit was personalised and numbered. Everybody knew which kit was theirs, and theirs alone.

It was not so much that the players were pampered, simply that the club took a professional attitude towards them. In return they demanded a considerable commitment.

The training, for example, was meticulously planned and quite hard, but it was excellent, with most of the emphasis on ball skills. What's more, everybody had a ball each.

At Manchester United there was none of that. It was still the Dark Ages. We were lucky if we had five balls for the whole team. When we came in for training, they slung

Pat Crerand: *My first P60 signed by Manchester United secretary Les Olive, showing my total earnings for 1962-63. The section for previous employment referred, of course, to Celtic who had paid me up until the beginning of February.*

The changing face of Old Trafford during the 1960s: a major facelift underway in July 1963 **(top)** *and stand improvements* **(above)** *in 1965 in preparation for the World Cup the following year.*

a pile of old jerseys on the table and you had to sort through it like at a jumble sale and try and pick out one that fitted you and was not totally falling apart. On a good day you might get one which only had a big hole in the sleeve, and a decaying tracksuit to go with it.

If you wanted a pair of boots, they looked at you as if you were asking for the moon. If you wanted a second pair of boots, forget it.

It was the same with the dressing-rooms. When we went to Real Madrid, or Benfica, and we saw all those individual baths laid out for all the players, we used to ask ourselves, 'I wonder what they think when they come to our place.'

Denis Law: *The changing facilities were a bit more basic in those days. David Herd is already changed for training so it looks as though I am probably late again.*

At Old Trafford the facilities changed very little in the period we are talking about. The ground changed, in preparation for the World Cup matches that were played there in 1966. But the basic facilities remained poor – more fit for horses than men. Today's players would certainly have looked down their noses at the Old Trafford of, say, 1965. Despite all that, it was a great time to be playing professional football. For the first time since the war life had become easier for a lot of people. People were buying themselves things they had never had before, like a television set, or a washing machine or a car.

It was also the time when football was starting to lose its old image of the bloke with a cloth cap and rattle, and to be seen as entertainment as well as a great game. You had the new music scene too. The Beatles, the Rolling Stones and all those other groups had come through, and public attitudes were generally loosening up. Quite enough has been said already about the Swinging Sixties, but it is true to say that we as footballers felt we were part of that scene.

It was a happy time to be young and enjoy what you were doing. Relations between rival clubs and their spectators were also much friendlier than they are now. The First Division was a far more open competition, and you didn't have that gulf between the very big super-rich clubs and the rest.

In a 1960s season, any one of eight clubs could have won the title, and there were always others who might spring a few surprses and get themselves into contention.

Today you expect the Premiership title to go to one of about four clubs – United, Liverpool, Newcastle United and Arsenal – and nobody else really gets a look-in. But in the Sixties we had a whole lot more title-winners, and it changed about from year to year.

Left *Win or lose West Ham were always an enjoyable fixture. Here Geoff Hurst leaps to avoid David Gaskell at Upton Park in 1964.*
Below *We also had our share of ups and downs against Spurs. This was one of the bad days, a 5-1 defeat at White Hart Lane in October 1965. The three men you can see going for the ball are Tottenham centre-half Laurie Brown, Bill Foulkes and Bobby Charlton.*

It was very rare for one club to win the title twice on the bounce, and if you look at the records you find it was unusual for one club to win the Championship more than twice in a decade. If you won it at all, it meant you had won it against big competition from a lot of other sides. Between 1959-60 and 1969-70 the Champions were:

1959-60 Burnley	1965-66 Liverpool
1960-61 Tottenham Hotspur	1966-67 Manchester United
1961-62 Ipswich Town	1967-68 Manchester City
1962-63 Everton	1968-69 Leeds United
1963-64 Liverpool	1969-70 Everton
1964-65 Manchester United	

At United we took pride in the kind of open football we played and the teams we most enjoyed playing against shared our attitude: Tottenham, West Ham and Liverpool were the main ones.

We always had a great rivalry with Liverpool. Nine times out of ten we beat them at Old Trafford, but we always got stuffed at Anfield. We were big pals with their players, and the managers too were great friends. Matt Busby and Bill Shankly each took a terrific interest in what the other was doing. If Liverpool did not have a game, and we were at home, you would find Shankly in our directors' box with his red shirt on and his red tie. Daft as it may sound, he used to love Manchester United.

Appeals for offside, but George Best plays on against old rivals Liverpool in October 1964.

Afterwards we had a drink with the Liverpool players, and the spectators always seemed to enjoy themselves, never mind the result. Today the spectators dislike each other intensely – and that is putting it very mildly. They hate each other, and the atmosphere is diabolical.

Pat Crerand: It was never like that. One year, when Liverpool were in the Cup Final, I went to watch the match on television with Denis and Noel Cantwell at the house of a friend called John Hogan. Liverpool won 2-1, against Leeds, and we were delighted for them. Ian St John, especially, was a great friend of mine and we all loved Bill Shankly. As soon as the game was finished we sent him a telegram to congratulate him and the team. They had never won the Cup before and we were just simply happy for them.

We were out of our seats when Ian St John scored against Leeds in the 1966 Cup Final.

One club that brought a lot of edge into the game was Leeds United. That is not to say they were responsible for everything that started to spoil football at the end of the Sixties – the mob fights and the gangs and all that. They did not invent the skinheads, for one thing – they were a kind of London invention. But, as players, we always had our suspicions about them.

When you played Leeds you knew they would try on extra things to needle you – little things, but always very close to the line, and often on the wrong side of it. The pity of it was that they didn't have to, because they were a great team and had a lot of great players. Probably this extra aggression came from Don Revie, the manager, who built them up from a Second Division side into a team capable of winning the double. It was strange, because Don himself had been a very creative player with Manchester City and England.

The other thing we remember about Leeds was that their goalkeeper, Gary Sprake, always played a blinder against us. Gary had a lot of criticism in his career, and it is true he could be erratic, but if you only saw a video of his matches against Manchester United you would think he was the finest goalkeeper God ever created.

To be fair, you cannot put all the blame for aggression on one club. It was part of the way the game was played, and how British referees interpreted the rules. It was a simple fact that every leading club with two or three really good players also had a couple who knew how to look after themselves.

In our team we had Bill Foulkes and Nobby Stiles. Nobby was never the largest man on the field but he was a tremendous battler and could be extremely single-minded. If he wanted the ball, or somebody needed to be tackled – bang! – he went for it.

At Leeds they had Billy Bremner – a little Scottish boy – Norman Hunter, Big Jack Charlton. At Spurs they had Dave Mackay, who was like a tank, and Maurice Norman at centre-half. At Liverpool there was Tommy Smith and Big Ron Yeats. Ron Harris at Chelsea, and Eddie McCreadie.

For an attacking player the list was endless. But in those days you gave as well as you took. That was understood. If you got kicked, you knew you could get in some retaliation without the whole thing turning sour or leading into a punch-up. Of course we had our arguments, but in the main the game was played fairly and with respect. You didn't have players taking dives as soon as somebody looked at them.

In return, the referees let the game flow and you did not have as many stoppages as you get today, nor half the number of penalty-kicks. In the Sixties it was very different, especially for the forwards. If the ball was played up to the front man, the opposing centre-half just kicked everything – ball, legs, anything he could connect with. Tackling from behind was not illegal and you had to take the blows, pick yourself up and start playing again.

If you objected, or took a swing at the guy who had tackled you, then you could be sure of trouble. In our experience it was the bad guy, or the instigator, who got away with it and the retaliator, the one who hit back, who ended up in the book or was sent off.

Denis Law: *Pat does his best to plead my case to referee Peter Rhodes after an incident at Blackpool in 1964, but I am already on my way. He was also there to support me at the hearing along with Matt Busby, David Herd and PFA secretary Cliff Lloyd, but I still got a 28-day suspension and a fine of £50.*

It was really difficult. On the one hand you had the rules of the game, which everybody was supposed to know and follow, or be punished, and on the other hand you had to look after yourself. If someone kicked you, and you did nothing about it, well then, he'd won the battle. You had to get back at him and make him think twice before he tried it again. Otherwise he'd kick you all over the place for 90 minutes.

Matt Busby had a sensible attitude to this. He understood the problem, and in his talk before the game he would come to this particular individual and then say, 'Let him know that you're there.' It was very shrewd of him, because he left it to the player to interpret things any way he liked. We knew, at the same time, that both he and Jimmy Murphy expected a real commitment from us, and that we would get a flea in the ear if we didn't provide it.

This was the year we almost made the leap from a potentially good side to a great one. After Tottenham had won the Double of League and FA Cup in 1960-61, this was the target to which all other clubs aspired.

In the mid-Sixties there were three main contenders – United, Liverpool and Leeds United, who were promoted from the Second Divison in 1964 and immediately joined the challenge for top honours.

We were also in contention for a third trophy, the Inter-Cities Fairs Cup, and made steady progress through the season.

Right	LIVERPOOL (Red Jerseys)			Left

LAWRENCE (I)

LAWLER (2)   BYRNE (3)

MILNE (4)   YEATS (5)   STEVENSON (6)

CALLAGHAN (7)   HUNT (8)   ST. JOHN (9)   GRAHAM (10)   THOMPSON (11)

Referee:
Mr. J. K. Taylor
(Wolverhampton)

Linesmen:
Mr. J. Tracey (Red Flag)
Mr. J. K. Wright
(Yellow Flag)

BEST (II)   LAW (10)   HERD (9)   CHARLTON (8)   CONNELLY (7)

STILES (6)   FOULKES (5)   CRERAND (4)

DUNNE, A. (3)   BRENNAN (2)

DUNNE, P. (1)

Left   **MANCHESTER UNITED** (Blue Jerseys)   Right

Liverpool were one of our main rivals in the Sixties and it was an impressive side that they put out against us at Anfield in October 1964.

In April 1964 Matt Busby signed winger John Connelly from Burnley and he rounded out our attack, giving it a balance we had previously lacked. We made a slow start in the League but then had a run of 14 matches in which we scored 27 out of 28 points (2 points for a win in those days).

By the New Year we had been through a lull and were three points behind Leeds after they had beaten us 1-0 on a horrible foggy day at Old Trafford. After that

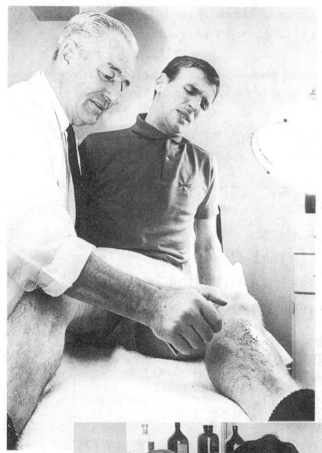

everybody knew what a good team they were, and they remained a constant threat for the rest of the decade and beyond.

Leeds stayed on top of the League until the middle of April. Then we went to Elland Road and took our revenge through a goal by John Connelly. All our games against Leeds were tough, and this one was no exception. On their side, they had gained the advantage over us in the Cup, beating us in a semi-final replay. The first game, at Hillsborough, had been a bad-tempered brawl with several players getting involved in a spectacular dust-up. In a well-known

Pat Crerand: *European opposition was always fierce and I needed six stitches after this Inter-Cities Fairs Cup-tie at Old Trafford in 1964. Ted Dalton checks the damage and* **(below)** *examines Tony Dunne's injured ankle. George Best looks concerned but heaven knows what Denis is up to in the background.*

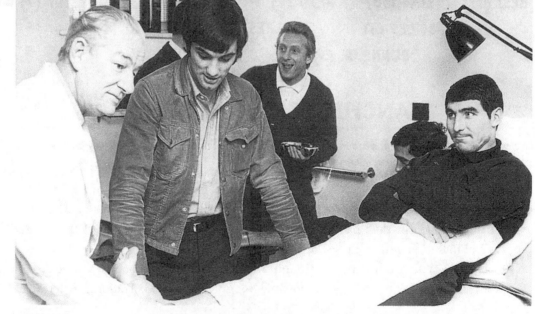

press photo, Billy Bremner is at the centre of things, apparently about to be strangled by three United players wearing the numbers 10, 4 and 6 on their shirts.

That match was scoreless, but in the replay we were all over them. The ball was hitting the woodwork and bouncing off Gary Sprake after he was well beaten. There seemed to be no way the ball would go into the net until three minutes from time when the back of Billy Bremner's head came into contact with a cross and it went in. Exit United.

In the League, however, we held them off. A 3-1 victory over Arsenal in the penultimate match secured it for us. Leeds could only draw 3-3 at Birmingham and we took the Championship on goal average. For the first time in nine years we had qualified for the European Cup.

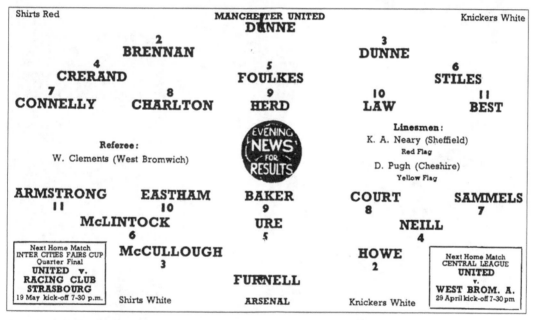

The two teams as per programme for the vital game against Arsenal at the end of the 1964-65 season.

Pat Crerand: Ted Dalton was our physio. He was a lovely man, a charmer. You'd believe anything he told you, even if you knew it couldn't be true. For that Arsenal match Denis was totally unfit and should never have played. But Ted and Matt kidded him on and made him play – and he scored twice. He should never have been on the field at all.

Denis Law: The treatment we used to receive was very basic. A cold sponge on the pitch, a bit of heat and a rub-down in the treatment room. I was in agony for five or six years because of a knee problem, but none of the experts seemed to get anywhere with it. Today I could have had an operation and been back playing, fully cured, inside a fortnight.

As it was, I was pouring cold water on it from a hosepipe before a game. Ridiculous. And all the time the club was egging you on to play when you really should not have gone near the pitch.

Denis Law: *The game is over and, from the bottles on the table, the celebrations have begun but my knee is in need of serious attention from Ted Dalton at the end of the Arsenal game. David Herd (left) and Matt Busby's son Sandy inspect the damage.*

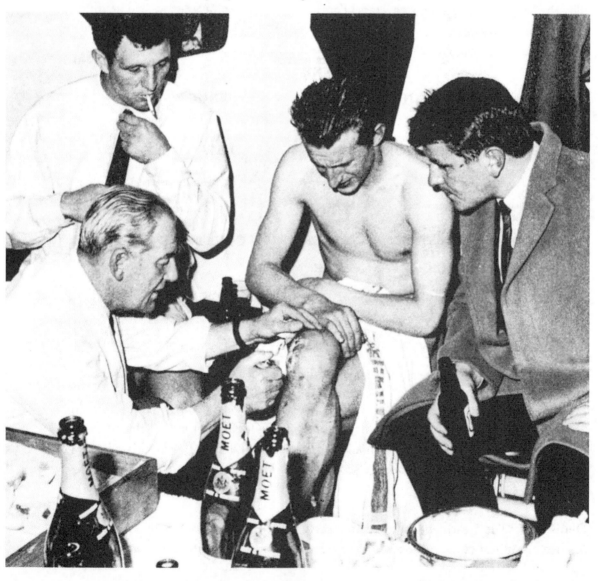

The Saturday before the Arsenal game I had got a a a bad gash on the knee which needed seven stitches in it. On the Monday I went in for treatment and was just hobbling along past the offices when Matt Busy came out.

'Where are you going?' he asked me. 'It's time for the team talk.'

'What do you mean?' I said. 'I can't possibly play tonight. I've got seven stitches in my knee.'

'You can play,' he said. 'You'll be all right. We'll get it strapped up.'

And that was what happened. They strapped the knee up really tight, the stitches stayed in place, and although it was stiff to run on I got through the game. Looking back, I can understand that Matt wanted to put out his first-choice formation for a key match like that. But there was no way I should have played.

It would have been a marvellous crowner to the season if we had won the Inter-Cities Fairs Cup. We cleared the first three rounds with aggregate victories over Djurgaarden, Sweden (7-2),

Overleaf *Holders of the Championship Trophy and the Charity Shield (shared with Liverpool after a 2-2 draw in August 1965). Back row (left to right): Nobby Stiles, Tony Dunne, David Gaskell, Harry Gregg, Pat Crerand, John Fitzpatrick. Middle row: Jack Crompton, Shay Brennan, David Sadler, Bill Foulkes, John Aston, Noel Cantwell, Matt Busby. Front row: John Connelly, Bobby Charlton, David Herd, Denis Law, George Best.*

Manchester United are champions

Arsenal fight hard but vainly

By ERIC TODD : Manchester U. 3, Arsenal 1

Manchester United, understandably perhaps, made rather heavy weather of their last home game of the season against Arsenal last night. Nevertheless their victory 3-1, allied to Leeds United's draw at Birmingham, means that the footballing championship title has come back to Old Trafford after an almost reluctant absence of eight years.

Under the circumstances, it would be pointless to dwell too long on a critical analysis of last night's game, for the atmosphere was charged with expectation and not a little apprehension on and off the field. Not ideal conditions under which to play with so much at stake, and Arsenal were in no mood to be charitable or even co-operative. There was no reason why they should have been.

Arsenal, indeed, played some excellent football, particularly in the second half, but they found Stiles, Brennan, and A. Dunne in brilliant form. The Arsenal defenders generally had the measure of some erratic play by United's forwards, although they never had it of Law, who with one sound leg still looked more dangerous and at the same time as skilful as any others who were in full possession of their physical faculties. Law has had his critics in recent weeks, but he remains one of the most inspired and inspiring players in the business. He has been a fine captain of a fine team which has won the title on merit.

Good news

Whatever it was going to be like later on, the early news was greeted with satisfaction by United supporters. Herd was fit again, and Law also was among those present in spite of having his right knee bandaged as a result of an injury received against Liverpool. And with the game only six minutes old Law supplied the pass from which Best put United in front. Best took his chance well, trapping the ball as it bounced awkwardly and driving it home almost in the same movement.

Eastham tried hard to instil some powers of retaliation into his forwards and Arsenal forced two corners, but there was no real danger to United, who might have scored a second goal if Best, having taken the ball off Neill, had not run out of steam at the end of a splendid run. Then a shot by Herd was deflected luckily for a corner. It was all United and Arsenal were indebted to Ure and Howe for some cool relief work under persistent if not always lethal pressure.

Arsenal, however, were dangerous in breakaways and P. Dunne went down full length and saved a good shot by Sammels after smart interpassing with Court. This was the prelude to a heavy assault by Arsenal, and now it was United's turn to look harassed in spite of the intelligence from St Andrews that Leeds were a goal down.

All forgiven

A slovenly start to the second half was relieved only by a superb pass by Law to A. Dunne, who did all that was required of him, but when he centred, none of his colleagues showed any initiative in taking up station. All was forgiven in the sixtieth minute, however, when, after Herd had headed the ball against the crossbar, Law beat Furnell from close in. What with this and the tidings of Leeds's harsh treatment at Birmingham, the Stretford end was justified in giving itself up to songs of praise and thanksgiving.

The songsters, nevertheless, were silent in the sixty-sixth minute when Crerand tripped Baker in the penalty area. P. Dunne, diving to his right, made a magnificent save from Eastham's penalty kick—but he could not hold the ball and Eastham, following up, scored easily. All was well in the end, for although Arsenal fought hard, United scored a third goal with minutes to go. Best took a corner kick, Howe missed the ball, and with Furnell unsighted, the irrepressible Law shot it into the net. And so United, with the same number of points as Leeds but with a better goal average go to Aston Villa tomorrow night as champions and worthy champions at that.

MANCHESTER UNITED. — Dunne (P.): Brennan, Dunne (A.); Crerand, Foulkes, Stiles; Connelly, Charlton, Herd, Law, Best. ARSENAL.—Furnell; Howe, McCullough; Neill, Ure, McLintock; Sammels, Court, Baker, Eastham, Armstrong.

Referee: W. Clements (West Bromwich).

Borussia Dortmund, West Germany (10-1) and a tough double encounter with Everton (3-2). Then we beat Racing Strasbourg, France by 5-0 and were drawn against Ferencvaros of Hungary in the semi-final.

We beat them 3-2 at home and lost 1-0 away. That put us level on aggregate, and under the rules then in force we had to go for a replay. A coin was tossed for home advantage and we lost. This meant we had to trail back to Budapest in the middle of June. We lost 2-1. In less than a month we would have to start training again for the next season.

By getting so far in two big Cup competitions we had stretched ourselves to the limits. In addition to the 42 matches of the League programme we had played seven FA Cup matches (including 2 replays) and 11 European matches (1 replay). That was a total of 60 important matches in 42 weeks.

After the defeat by Ferencvaros, one football writer wrote about Manchester United 'confirming the fears of those who believed their organisation hardly matched their talent.' It is all right for journalists, but if he had had our injuries, and our mental exhaustion, he probably could not have carried his typewriter upstairs, let alone play 60 first-class football matches.

Pat Crerand: People said it wasn't too much to play 60 or 70 games a season. It may be hard work, they said, but what about the lads who went down the mines every day? Yes, that was all very well, but the lads who went down the mines didn't have 60,000 people to give them a bollocking every time they dropped a bit of coal!

Top *We always used to entertain our European visitors after a game and this is the menu produced by the Midland Hotel for the meal after our Inter-Cities Fairs Cup game against Borussia Dortmund in 1964. We beat them 10-1 on aggregate. Little did we realise that the same club would be back at Old Trafford over thirty later to ruin United's chance of a second European Cup in the 1997 semi-final.*

Denis Law: *The end of a long season and we were both selected to play for Scotland against England at Wembley. Here I am (above) on the empty Wembley terraces on the eve of the match.*

In the 1960s there was a tactical revolution in the English game, a lot of which was started by us at United. We were in Europe every season between 1963-64 and 1968-69 and this called for special tactics, especially away from home where it was important to hold the opposition and not give away goals.

Some of our style was modelled on what the European clubs did, but most of it was designed to make the most of our particular playing strengths. We began by moving away from the old standard line-up of two full-backs, then a three-man half-back row and five forwards. Once we had the partnership of Nobby Stiles the ball-winner and Pat, who was the creative force, we were able to try out a whole set of new moves.

Nobby had the old wing-half's number 6 on his jersey but he played further back with Bill Foulkes who was more of a central defender. Pat and Bobby Charlton were in front of them as the midfield links, and up front there was Denis and David Herd as central strikers. That was the core of the team, and out on the flanks we had the full-backs and the wingers.

When Alf Ramsey brought in his 4-3-3 'wingless wonders' formation, and won the World Cup with it, a lot of clubs followed his example. We did not. We kept our wing men to give us that extra flexibility in attack which Matt Busby thought was so important. The drawback with the Ramsey formation was that it did not work unless

Denis Law: *They were were an ideal partnership, Pat was a sweet passer of the ball and Nobby was one of the all-time great ball-winners.*

Two defenders who never spent too much time in their opponents' half of the field - Tony Dunne **(above left)** *and Shay Brennan* **(above right)**.

you had flank players capable of doing two jobs at once – doubling back in defence and belting up the wing as far as the other corner flag and then crossing the ball for your strikers. Playing that way meant you were always liable to be caught out somewhere in the middle, and then were unable to get back.

In any case, we did not have flank players. We had Tony Dunne and Shay Brennan, and they were defenders. Tony Dunne could not cross the ball to save his life and Shay Brennan never had the energy to get as far as their corner flag. The way we played it, we relied on proper wingers to do the running and crossing. We had Bestie on one side of the field and sometimes Bobby also played out wide. Then we had John Connelly, followed by Johnny Aston, who were both out-and-out wingers, and then Willie Morgan came into the side.

Up front we were always flexible. If the marking was tight, and we were not getting anywhere, we used to flit about. Bestie would pop up inside or on the other wing and Denis would also go roaming. That way you could confuse their defenders, or drag them

Facing page *The wingers: John Connelly (top left), Willie Morgan (top right) and John Aston in action against Liverpool.*

No chance for John Charles of West Ham as he is outnumbered by Jimmy Ryan, Nobby Stiles and Bill Foulkes.

Pat Crerand: *Three examples of Denis's lethal finishing from close range.*

out of position and make an opening for someone else to come through. When clubs started marking us man-for-man, as Arsenal did, then we drew back and let them follow us. They, however, did not like coming too far because this left space behind them for Bobby to come charging in on a through ball.

Both David Herd and Bobby had tremendous shots from any range, able to pounce on any gap that showed itself, and Bestie could fire them in from all sorts of angles.

Denis Law: As soon as I saw a long-range shot going in, I would be in the middle closing on the goalkeeper. I picked up a lot of goals this way because I knew there was always a chance the goalkeeper would not be able to hold the ball. David and Bobby hit their shots so hard, the ball arrived that fraction of a second sooner and goalkeepers were often struggling to get across in time, let alone catch the ball cleanly. If they dropped it, and it fell a yard or two away from them, I was in to nick it off them and put it in the net.

It was generally the most adventurous sides who got the best out of this kind of flexible attacking system. Before us, the great Spurs team did it too. They had Cliff Jones and Terry Medwin changing places on the wings, John White travelling all over the place to create moves, and Jimmy Greaves and big Bobby Smith to finish things off in the middle in their own completely different styles: Bobby the poacher and Jimmy the footballing genius who could make his own goals out of nothing.

Pat Crerand: *Bill Foulkes and I battle it out in one of our close-fought games against Spurs, while David Gaskell waits on his line.*

Matt Busby was never a great one for detailed tactics. Of course we had our plans for this and that opponent and special moves for corner-kicks and so on. But mostly we did not use the blackboard unless something had really gone wrong – then out came the board and the bag of magnetic discs.

In general Matt's message was, 'Go out and play your football.' He knew he had skilful players, and he simply asked them to use their heads and be adaptable within the framework of his broad tactical plan. Provided we did that, and kept on trying for the full 90 minutes, then he reckoned the goals would come. Now that we were secure at the back, and not leaking goals as we had been doing, then the results should be in our favour more often than not.

Above it all, Matt Busby had his vision of a side that would be successful not just at home but in Europe too. And in our minds there was also the image of the great 1950s side. We always felt we had to try and get ourselves up to their level and give the people of Manchester the success they were looking for.

We tried it by playing exciting football. We did not try to go out and get results by defending, we went out to do it by attacking. Matt always said, 'Keep at it. Keep trying. Even if you are two goals down, take the game to them. Don't give up. Something will happen.' In Europe we learned we had to play it differently, especially on the away leg, but most of the time we set out to entertain the people.

In the 1966-67 season we went out of the FA Cup in the fourth round, beaten 2-1 at home by Norwich City. It was an unbelievable shock result, especially for us as we had got at least as far as the semi-final for the last five seasons.

People say, 'Well, it's a good thing to get knocked out early.' It isn't. It is never a good thing to be knocked out of a competition early because once you start out you always want to win everything.

The previous year we had also reached the semi-final of the European Cup (see 'Going for Europe'), but in the League we had finished fourth so now we were not in Europe at all – our first break from European competition for three years.

Not too many names in this Norwich side that are remembered by more than the Carrow Road regulars, but they were good enough to put us out of the Cup at Old Trafford in 1967.

Sweet dreams for Norwich, nightmare for United

By PAUL FITZPATRICK : Manchester United 1, Norwich City 2

"It's going to be a nightmare" said Laurie Brown, the Norwich City centre half, to his wife on the eve of the Manchester United-Norwich FA Cup game at Old Trafford. "They will probably score a record number of goals or something. I don't fancy it one bit." Neither Brown nor his colleagues experienced a nightmare. Rather, at twenty minutes to five, the Norwich players must have felt that they were floating on pink, fluffy clouds. They had beaten Manchester United 2-1.

This result must seem eerie to those who do not believe in impossibilities. But Norwich, and deservedly so, achieved the impossible. True, the ball for most of the time was in and around the Norwich penalty area. True, too, United had more class and individual skill. But let not the United supporters weep any crocodile tears over this defeat. Norwich's forwards took advantage of two bad errors by United's defence and scored twice. Then, when Norwich had to defend, as they did for most of the game, they defended superbly. Lucas, Brown, Allcock, and Keelan were magnificent. "Oh, how the lads fought," said Brown. They did, too !

Best, that wayward genius, was in one of his most wayward moods and his troubles epitomised United's for they were a fitful, fretful, disjointed, unhappy side. Ryan seemed to regard the ball

as a personal treasure and something not to be parted with at any price. Charlton rolled down his socks after half time but still contributed nothing to the game. Herd was shackled.

United's only crumbs of comfort were the performances of Dunne, Sadler, and Stepney who were impeccable, and Law who was brilliant. Indeed, when Law had the ball United had a chance. He scored an equalising goal for United and, among all the fine goals that have been scored at Old Trafford over the years, this surely was one of the finest. Law tried everything he knew to bring United victory. Law was United's forward line.

After 25 minutes Brown pushed the ball to Bryceland whose pass caught United's defence strung across the field like washing on a line. Heath was set free and he beat Stepney easily. United equalised ten minutes later when Law began and completed a move which also involved Ryan. It would be impertinent to try to describe this goal in detail. I could not do it justice. It was a masterpiece, no less.

Norwich's decisive goal came in the sixty-fifth minute after Stiles and Dunne had got themselves mixed up over a pass back to Stepney. Bolland was given the simple and enjoyable task of shovelling the last mound of earth over United's coffin.

MANCHESTER UNITED.—Stepney; Dunne, Noble; Crerand, Sadler, Stiles; Ryan, Law, Charlton, Herd, Best.

NORWICH CITY.—Keelan; Stringer, Mullett; Lucas, Brown, Allcock; Kenning, Heath, Bryceland, Bolland, Anderson.

Referee: W J Gow (Swansea)

MANCHESTER UNITED		NORWICH CITY
Shirts : Red Shorts : White		Shirts : Yellow and Green Shorts : Black
1 STEPNEY	**REFEREE :** W. J. Gow (Swansea)	KEELAN 1
2 DUNNE (A)		STRINGER 2
3 NOBLE		MULLETT 3
4 CRERAND		LUCAS 4
5 FOULKES		BROWN 5
6 STILES		ALLCOCK 6
7 BEST	**LINESMEN :**	KENNING 7
8 LAW	G. H. Morris (Blackheath) *(Red Flag)*	BRYCELAND 8
9 SADLER	D. Turner (Rugeley, Staffs.) *(Yellow Flag)*	SHEFFIELD 9
10 HERD		BOLLAND 10
11 CHARLTON		ANDERSON 11
S.		HEATH S.

BUY THE FOOTBALL PINK

Next Home Match
1st DIVISION
UNITED
v.
BLACKPOOL
● 25th Feb. kick-off 3-00

Next Home Match
CENTRAL LEAGUE
UNITED
v.
ASTON VILLA
● 4th March kick-off 3-00

Alex Stepney arrives in Manchester to replace Harry Gregg **(right)** *and* **(far right)** *goes into action against Liverpool.*

So there it was. Like it or not, we had no more Cup games and we could concentrate on the League. We did not have all those midweek fixtures to play, and for us that was a big change.

Early in the season we lost John Connelly who went to Blackburn Rovers. The players were sorry to see him go, but perhaps he was having to pay for two indifferent semi-final matches the previous year, against Partizan Belgrade in the European Cup and against Everton in the FA Cup.

Into his place came John Aston, a left-sided player who went out on the left wing. Bestie could play on either side of the field, although he was naturally a right-footed player. He switched over to the other wing and we kept our basic 4-2-4 formation.

In goal Harry Gregg had been having injury problems, most of all from a bad shoulder which kept popping out when he stretched for a ball. We went on a pre-season tour and got thumped all over the place – 4-1 by Celtic, 4-1 by Bayern Munich and 5-2 by FK Austria. Harry's career was unfortunately in jeopardy, and later that season he was transferred to Stoke. It was sad because Harry was a brave player who had joined United in 1957, crawled uninjured out of the Munich air crash and had been a first-team regular more or less ever since.

David Gaskell came in for him, but when David was injured soon afterwards Matt Busby went into the transfer market and bought Alex Stepney from Chelsea. Alex had only been there a short time, having made

his name in the Third Division with Millwall. Then Chelsea wanted him as cover because they thought Peter Bonnetti was leaving, but then he stayed and Chelsea did not need the two of them. It was a gamble for United to buy him but Alex proved himself quickly enough. He was a smashing goalkeeper.

In the first part of the season we had an up-and-down record, but by mid-December we had sorted ourselves out. From then on we had a great unbeaten run of 20 League matches without defeat.

That was Championship stuff and by the middle of March we were at the top of the table. We had a bad setback a week later when David Herd broke his leg while scoring a goal against Leicester. He stuck out his leg to toe-poke the ball past Gordon Banks and the leg was somehow wedged between Gordon's body and Graham Cross who was running in from the side to tackle him. When the leg went, a terrible crack like a pistol shot went all round Old Trafford.

It was not the complete end of David's career as he made a comeback the following season, but after that he did not continue in the side for much longer. Like Harry he moved to Stoke and later went into management.

David Herd's replacement was David Sadler, a utility player whose main position was at centre-half. He settled in well up front and stayed in our formation for the rest of the season.

Denis Law: *The game against West Ham that decided the Championship included this almost unique contribution from Pat, as he gets up to a cross ahead of Bobby Charlton to score in the first half.*

With two matches to go we needed two points to win the title. We had to play West Ham away and Stoke City at home.

Pat Crerand: We went down to Upton Park and I'll never forget it because I scored with a header, which is a miracle on its own. But the funny thing about that game was Matt Busby missing the start.

Matt came down to the side of the pitch and got there just as West Ham were kicking off. But Matt did not realise that we had already scored with about the first kick of the ball. For some reason he had been held up in the dressing-room and when he got down to the pitch he thought West Ham were kicking off to start the match.

The Championship is ours and the champagne is out in the visitors' dressing room at Upton Park.

Denis Law: *I didn't play in the final game of the season against Stoke but was on the pitch beforehand for the formal presentation of the Championship trophy.*

Below *Matt Busby joins the team in a lap of thanks to the Old Trafford fans and Bill Foulkes holds aloft the Championship trophy.*

Holders of the Championship Trophy and the Charity Shield. Back row (left to right): Noel Cantwell, David Sadler, David Herd, Bill Foulkes, Jimmy Ryan, Jack Crompton. Middle row: David Gaskell, Shay Brennan, Bobby Charlton, John Aston, Pat Crerand, Alex Stepney. Front row: John Fitzpatrick, Nobby Stiles, Tony Dunne, Matt Busby, Denis Law, George Best, Bobby Noble.

At half-time he thought it was 2-0 for us and we were really leading 3-0. Once he realised, he was a lot more relaxed. Sometimes, when you have only a 2-0 lead, the manager will say, 'Just keep it tight for the first ten minutes and kill the game off.'

But when you are three goals up you can charge the opposition. We went after West Ham in the second half and finished up winning the Championship with a 6-1 victory.

It was a great win and we had a lot of praise for it. West Ham were not an easy side – they had a skilful footballing team with Bobby Moore, Geoff Hurst and Martin Peters. The press raved about our ability and Matt was very pleased too. Most of the time he would not give the press anything, but after that game he told them it was 'my finest hour'. They loved it.

I remember another, silly thing that happened the night before the game. We went down to London on the afternoon train and then seven or eight of us went to the pictures at one of the big cinemas in Leicester Square. Somehow we always conned David Herd into paying for the tickets. We were in the foyer and this time it was me who had to get the sweets.

So Denis goes up to the counter and says to the lass, 'I'll have that box of chocolates up there.'

She fetches it down and it costs three quid! Three quid was an astronomical amount of money in those days. But I couldn't back down. It finished up with me paying out about twenty quid for sweets.

And did they eat them? No way. They saved them up and took them home to their wives.

End of season celebrations for the League Champions. Another banquet at the Midland Hotel and the official souvenir brochure.

A
BANQUET
*to commemorate the winning of
The League Championship
Season 1966-67
by
Manchester United Football Club*

The Midland Hotel · Manchester
August 4th 1967

MANCHESTER UNITED F.C.

2/6

PLAYERS OFFICIAL
SOUVENIR OF
CHAMPIONSHIP
1966—67

When we first started playing at United, life was much simpler than it is today. Travel was not exactly horse-drawn but people did not have cars and few went on big journeys. Package holidays to Spain did not really get going until the late Sixties, and most people still went to a seaside resort in Britain and travelled there by train.

As for local transport, you took the bus, or the trolley bus, or whatever. Even if you had just scored the winning goal against Liverpool, it was still quite normal to go home on the bus. You can't imagine Alan Shearer doing that, or Ryan Giggs. It would be thought very strange – what's he up to? – but then it was completely normal.

Then, during the Sixties, people started to drive themselves to work in much larger numbers, and footballers did the same. The club also started to organise us a little more carefully. We went away on a Friday night before a game, and the whole approach became a lot more professional. If we had a match in London, we travelled first-class by train to Euston and stayed at the Russell Hotel which is about five minutes away.

It was very rare for us to fly, except when we had to go abroad. Then we went on scheduled flights only, no charters. To get to Amsterdam, for example, we flew down to London and then on to Amsterdam.

Because of the crash in 1958, flying was not a happy experience for many people in the club. It could be very quiet on the plane. Bobby, for one, was nervous, and it was very understandable. But it had to be done, there was no alternative. If the club was to keep to its League and Cup commitments, there was no other way to get there and back in time.

As things were, flying anywhere was a nightmare. What is now a 90-minute flight from Manchester used to take us 12 hours or more. Today a European match is just part of the weekly timetable – Madrid, Oslo, Vienna, Munich, no problem, get on the plane and go. You fly out there the day before and you come back as soon as it is over.

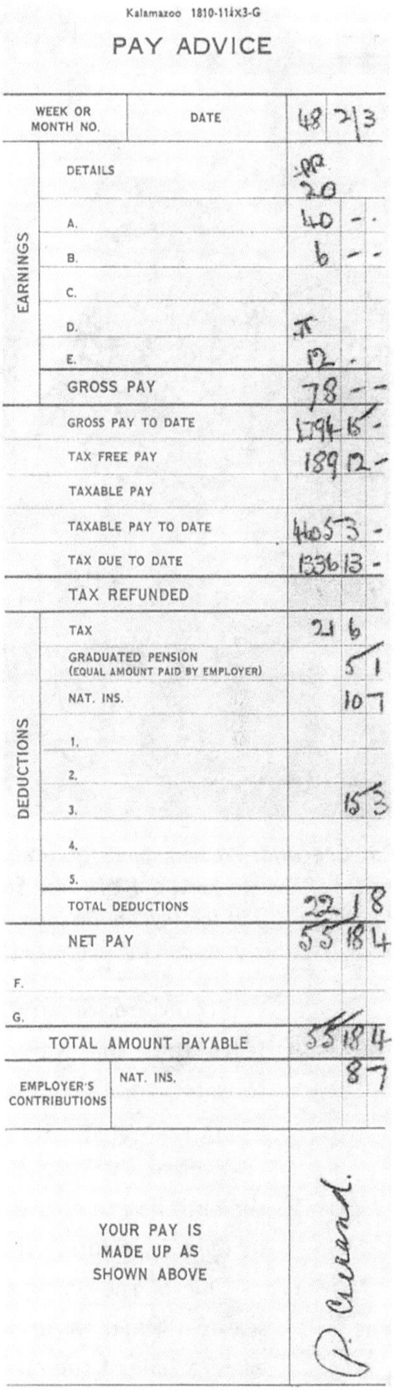

Pat Crerand: *Net take-home for the week, £55 18s 4d; even allowing for inflation this hardly compares with present rates in the Premiership!*

Kalamazoo 1810-11ix3-G

PAY ADVICE

WEEK OR MONTH NO.		DATE	48 2/3

EARNINGS	DETAILS	.pp 20
	A.	40 - .
	B.	6 - -
	C.	
	D.	π
	E.	12 .
	GROSS PAY	78 - -
	GROSS PAY TO DATE	1794 5 -
	TAX FREE PAY	189 12 -
	TAXABLE PAY	
	TAXABLE PAY TO DATE	4053 -
	TAX DUE TO DATE	1356 13 -
	TAX REFUNDED	
	TAX	21 6
	GRADUATED PENSION (EQUAL AMOUNT PAID BY EMPLOYER)	5 1
	NAT. INS.	10 7
DEDUCTIONS	1.	
	2.	
	3.	15 3
	4.	
	5.	
	TOTAL DEDUCTIONS	22 8
	NET PAY	55 18 4
	F.	
	G.	
	TOTAL AMOUNT PAYABLE	55 18 4
EMPLOYER'S CONTRIBUTIONS	NAT. INS.	8 7

YOUR PAY IS
MADE UP AS
SHOWN ABOVE

P. Crerand.

Pat Crerand: *Well-equipped for travel into the hard winter of Eastern Europe.* **Right** *Alex Stepney and I look knowledgeably at the sign on the snow-covered Gornik pitch.. Neither of us had the faintest idea what it said!*

Not then. We used to set off on the Monday morning around eight o'clock, spend all day travelling and hanging around in airports, arrive worn out at nine in the evening, see the ground the next day and do some training, then play the match.

Afterwards we went back to the hotel and had a few drinks. Matt Busby would come in with the directors and sit down with us. We'd have a bit of a sing-song and go to bed. Then it was home next morning, the Thursday. And every time you went anywhere with Manchester United, you came home at six o'clock in the morning. We could never understand it. Why couldn't we have a flight at, say, two in the afternoon? No chance. When it came to operations abroad, it was like being in the army.

Around 1963-64 none of us in the team knew much about Europe. We could not speak the languages, the food was not particularly great – especially behind the Iron Curtain, in East Germany, Poland or Hungary, where we played at various times – and we had to spend three days there.

Everybody else thought we were having a fantastic time. It was bloody awful. Before the game you had to train and keep yourself fit, so you could not do anything – no going out with the lads for a drink, nothing like that. It had to be that way, of course, and it still is. Today's players can at least find something to watch on Sky Television but in those days you could not watch television, or read the foreign newspapers, so most of the time you were bored out of your tree.

Eventually Matt Busby realised how tiring it was for everybody and accepted that the club had to change its ways. He was not convinced until the charter firms were able to show how much their standards had improved, and then we started to fly direct.

One of the worst trips was to East Berlin to play ASK Vorwaerts in the 1965-66 season. When we arrived at the border crossing at Checkpoint Charlie to go into the eastern half of the city, they kept us waiting for ages. Then we went through and the

16. Any other provisions:—
(Fill in as required).

17. In consideration of the observance by the said Player of the terms provisions and conditions of this Agreement, the said Robert Leslie Olive on behalf of the Club shall pay to the said Player the wages, bonuses and fees as provided hereinbefore and this Agreement (subject to the Rules of The Football Association) shall cease and terminate on the said 30th day of June, 1968 Unless either:
(a) This Agreement shall have previously been determined in accordance with the provisions of one or other of Clauses 10, 11 or 12 hereinbefore set forth; or
(b) The Club shall have before the last day of the playing season next preceding the said 30th day of June, 1968 by notice in writing to the Player continued this Agreement for a further period of two ~~year~~/years) (hereinafter called "the further period") on the same or not less favourable terms as to remuneration as provided in Clauses 15 and 16 hereof respectively and otherwise on the same terms as are expressed in and by this Agreement but excluding this option provision and so that such further period shall not be for longer in extent than that of the initial period of employment.

18. If the Club shall in pursuance of Clause 17(b) hereof continue this Agreement for a further period then and in that event this Agreement shall continue in full force and effect as between the parties hereto and shall terminate on the last day of such further period Unless either:
(a) This Agreement shall have been determined previously in accordance with the provisions of one or other of Clauses 10, 11 or 12 hereinbefore set forth; or
(b) The Club shall have before the last day of the playing season next preceding the last day of the further period of service by notice in writing to the Player indicate that the Club requires to offer a further re-engagement to the Player after the further period;
(c) If the Club shall have served notice on the Player of a renewed offer for his services, the Player shall then have the right to call upon the Club either to negotiate a new Contract of Service with him or to negotiate his transfer to another Club at an appropriate fee;
(d) The right of the Player given by Clause 18(c) hereof shall be exercised by him within 28 days of the notice given to him by the Club under Clause 18(b) hereof;
(e) In the event of the Club and the Player being unable by the last day of the further period to agree a new contract of service or to make arrangements for the transfer of the Player then either the Club or the Player shall be at liberty to exercise the rights of appeal contained in the Regulations of The Football League;
(f) Until an additional Contract of Service between the Club and Player becomes operative or the Player is transferred, either prior to or as the result of the determination of an appeal from either the Club or the Player, the Player's Contract of Service shall, after the Club shall have served notice on him under Sub-Clause 18(b) hereof be deemed to continue and have full force and effect between the parties thereto on the same terms as to remuneration and conditions of service as those obtaining prior to the expiration of the previous period of employment.

As Witness the hands of the said parties the day and year first aforesaid.

Signed by the said Robert Leslie Olive

and Patrick Timothy Crerand

(sgd) P. T. CRERAND
(Player)

in the presence of

(Signature) (sgd) A. Gaffney,

(Occupation) Typist,

(Address) Old Trafford, Manchester 16.

(sgd) R. L. OLIVE
(Secretary)

P/FL

COPY

An Agreement

made the First day of July, 19 66 between Robert Leslie Olive of Old Trafford, Manchester in the County of Lancashire the Secretary of and acting pursuant to Resolution and Authority for and on behalf of the MANCHESTER UNITED FOOTBALL CLUB of Manchester (hereinafter referred to as the Club) of the one part and PATRICK TIMOTHY CRERAND of 45, Erlington Avenue, Stretford, in the County of Lancashire Professional Football Player (hereinafter referred to as the Player) of the other part **Whereby** it is agreed as follows:—

1. The Player hereby agrees to play in an efficient manner and to the best of his ability for the Club for the period of two ~~year~~/years) (hereinafter called "the inital period of employment") from the First day of July, 1966 to the 30th day of June 1968. Unless the initial period of employment shall either be (a) previously determined in accordance with the provisions of one or other of Clauses 10, 11 or 12 hereof or (b) terminated extended or renewed as provided by Clauses 17 and 18 of this Agreement.

2. The Player shall attend the Club's ground or any other place decided upon by the Club for the purposes of or in connection with his training as a Player pursuant to the instructions of the Secretary, Manager, or Trainer of the Club, or of such other person, or persons as the Club may appoint.

3. The Player shall do everything necessary to get and keep himself in the best possible condition so as to render the most efficient service to the Club, and will carry out all the training and other instructions of the Club through its representative officials.

4. The Player shall observe and be subject to all the Rules, Regulations and Bye-Laws of The Football Association, and any other Association, League, or Combination of which the Club shall be a member. And this Agreement shall be subject to any action which shall be taken by The Football Association under their Rules for the suspension or termination of the Football Season, and if any such suspension or termination shall be decided upon the payment of wages shall likewise be suspended or terminated, as the case may be and in any proceedings by the Player against the Club it shall be a sufficient and complete defence and answer by and on the part of the Club that such suspension or termination hereof is due to the action of The Football Association, or any Sub-Committee thereof to whom the power may be delegated.

5. The Player shall not engage in any business or live in any place which the Directors (or Committee) of the Club may deem unsuitable.

6. Unless this Agreement has previously been determined by any one of Clauses 10, 11 or 12 hereof as hereinafter provided, the Player shall not before the last day of the playing season next preceding the expiration of any further or additional further period for which this Agreement shall have been renewed in accordance with the provisions of Clauses 17 or 18 hereof or before the last day of the playing season 19 68 if this Agreement shall not have been so renewed approach or entertain approaches from any other club or person with a view to changing his club unless otherwise agreed by the club and player. Under no circumstances shall the Player make any payment to agents or persons other than Clubs and persons regularly employed by Clubs and concerned in the engagement of Players with a view to obtaining employment.

7. The Player shall not directly or indirectly induce or attempt to induce a Player employed by another Club to leave that employment for any purpose or reason whatsoever.

8. The Player shall not offer to or receive from another Club or the Players of another Club or any person or organisation a bonus or any inducement to win lose or draw a match.

9. The Player may apply to The Football Association for a personal hearing to answer a charge of misconduct under F.A. Rule 38. He may also be represented at the hearing by the Professional Footballers' Association provided that such representative is not a member of the legal profession.

10. This Agreement may be terminated at any time by mutual consent of both Club and Player.

11. If the Player shall be guilty of serious misconduct or breach of the disciplinary Rules of the Club or of the terms and conditions of this Agreement, the Club may, on giving fourteen days' notice to the Player, terminate or suspend this Agreement in accordance with the Rules of The Football Association without prejudice to the Club's right to transfer fees, and such notice shall be in writing specifying the reason for the same being given. Provided that such notice shall set forth and the above power shall be subject to the Right of the Player to appeal as follows:—

Any League or other Combination of Clubs may, subject to these Rules make such regulations between their Clubs and Players as they may deem necessary. Where Leagues and Combinations are sanctioned direct by this Association an Appeals Committee shall be appointed by this Association. Where Leagues and Combinations are sanctioned by County Associations an Appeals Committee shall be appointed by the sanctioning County Associations. Where an agreement between a Club and a Player in any League or other Combination provides for the Club terminating by notice to the Player of the Agreement between the Club and Player on any reasonable ground the following practice shall prevail: A Player shall have the right to appeal to the Management Committee of his League or Combination and a further right of appeal to the Appeals Committee of that body. A Club on giving notice to a Player to terminate his Agreement must state in the notice the name and address of the Secretary of the League or Combination to which he may appeal, and must also at the same time give notice to the League or Combination of which the Club is a member. A copy of the notice sent to the Player must at the same time be forwarded to the Secretary of this Association. The Player shall have the right of appeal to the League or Combination, but such appeal must be made within 7 days of the receipt of the Notice from the Club. The Notice terminating the Agreement must inform the Player the reasons or grounds for such Notice. The appeal shall be heard by the Management Committee within 10 days of the receipt of the Notice from the Player. If either party is dissatisfied with the decision, there shall be a right of further appeal to the Appeals Committee of the League or Combination, but such appeal must be made within 7 days of receipt of the intimation of the decision of the Management Committee, and must be heard by the Appeals Committee within 10 days of the receipt of the Notice of Appeal.

The League or Combination shall report to this Association when the matter is finally determined, and the Agreement and Registration shall be cancelled by this Association where necessary. Agreements between Clubs and Players shall contain a clause showing the provision made for dealing with such disputes and for the cancelling of the Agreements and Registrations by this Association. Clubs not belonging to any League or Combination before referred to may, upon obtaining the approval of this Association, make similar regulations; such regulations to provide for a right of appeal by either party to the County Association, or to this Association.

12. In the event of the Club failing to fulfil the terms and conditions of this Agreement the Player may, on giving fourteen days' notice to the Club, terminate this Agreement, such notice to be in writing. The Player must forward a copy of the notice to The Football Association and the Club shall have the right of appeal within seven days to The Football Association, which may either dismiss such appeal, or allow the same, and, if so, on such terms and conditions as it may think fit.

13. The following special provisions laid down by the Competitions in which the Player will compete are accepted by and will be observed by the Player:—

(a) It is hereby agreed by the Player that if he shall at any time be absent from his duties by reason of sickness or injury he shall, during such absence, be entitled to receive only the difference between the weekly wage he was receiving at the time of his sickness or injury and the amount he receives as benefit under the National Insurance Act, 1946, or The National Insurance (Industrial Injuries) Act, 1946, and for the purpose of this Clause his wages shall be deemed to accrue from day to day.

(b) If at any time during the period of this Contract of Service the payments herein agreed shall be in excess of the payments permitted to be paid by the Club to the Player in accordance with Regulations 40(b), 41 and 44 of The Football League the payments to the player shall be the amount the Club is entitled to pay in accordance with such regulations and this Contract of Service shall be read and construed, as, if it were varied accordingly.

(c) The Player agrees that he will not without the written permission of the Club grant interviews to nor write articles for newspapers or other publications nor take part in television or radio programmes and that he will submit such articles etc. to the Club for approval before allowing publication of the same.

14. Basic Wages.

£65.0.0 per week from 1.7.1966 to 30.6.1968.
£______ per week from ______ to ______
£______ per week from ______ to ______
£______ per week from ______ to ______
£______ per week from ______ to ______
£______ per week from ______ to ______
£______ per week from ______ to ______
£______ per week from ______ to ______

15. Other financial provisions:—
(Fill in as required).

As per attached sheets.

Manchester United Football Club Ltd.

H. BUSBY, C.B.E. Manager   L. OLIVE, Secretary

TELEGRAPHIC ADDRESS:
STADIUM, MANCHESTER
TELEPHONE TRAFFORD PARK
1661 & 1662

Old Trafford,
Manchester, 16.

P. T. CRERAND

1. £ 65.0.0. per week basic wage.

2. When playing in the First Team you will receive:-
   (a) Match Bonus as laid down by Football League rule.
   (b) £20 per point Talent Money for points won in respect of every Football League match in which you play to be paid monthly.

3. In addition to the payments listed above the Club will pay bonuses as shown below to mark any success that may be achieved. The amounts shown will be divided amongst the players taking part pro-rata to the number of appearances made in the League Championship Competition.

Winners	£15,000
Runners Up	£ 9,900
Third Place	£ 6,600
Fourth Place	£ 4,400

4. When playing in Football Association cup-ties home or away:-
   (a) Appearance money will be paid as follows:-

Third Round	£ 40
Fourth Round	£ 50
Fifth Round	£ 75
Sixth Round	£125
Semi-Final	£200
Final	£400

   (b) Match bonus as allowed by Football League rule.
   (c) Talent money for winning F. A. Cup £6,000 to be divided amongst the players taking part, pro-rata to the number of appearances made in the competition.

5. If you are not selected for the First Team or unable to play through injury, you will receive your basic wage and half any point bonus payment made to members of the team for Football League games.

- 2 -

6. When playing in the European Champions Cup Competition the following payments will be made:-

	Appearance Money Each Game	Round Bonus
		£ 50
First Round	£ 25	£100
Second Round	£ 30	£250
Third Round	£ 50	£350
Fourth Round	£ 60	£500
Semi-Final	£ 75	£1000
Final	£125	
	(If only one match played - £250)	

7. When playing in European Cup Winners and Inter-Cities Fairs Cup Competitions, the following payments will be made.

	Appearance Money Each Game	Round Bonus
		£ 40
First Round	£ 20	£ 60
Second Round	£ 25	£100
Third Round	£ 35	£150
Fourth Round	£ 50	£300
Semi-Final	£ 70	£750
Final	£100	
	(If only one match played - £200)	

8. It is hereby agreed that on completion of five years employment with the Club a Service Bonus of £750 will be paid and that on completion of TEN years employment a further Service Bonus of £1,000 will be paid.

   It is further agreed that in the event of the Player being transferred to another Club before these periods of Service are completed, and always PROVIDING that this is to a Club of our choice and that you are not in dispute with Manchester United Football Club in any way, a sum equal to the amount accrued to the date of the transfer will be paid to you.

   In the event of you being granted a Free Transfer it is understood and agreed that you would not be entitled to receive any Accrued Share of the Service Bonus mentioned above.

- 3 -

9. In the event of you being transferred at the request of Manchester United Football Club, and to a Club of their choice, it is agreed that you will receive payment to the value of 2½% of any transfer fee received. It is understood and agreed that in the event of you being transferred at your own request for any reason whatsoever no percentage of any transfer fee received shall be payable to you.

10. OTHER COMPETITIONS

    In the event of the Club winning any other MAJOR FIRST TEAM Competitions(s) not listed above the Directors undertake to make available a sum of money, the amount to be decided at their discretion, for distribution pro-rata to the number of appearances.

11. GUARANTEE

    The Club hereby undertakes that notwithstanding the terms mentioned above, you will be guaranteed a MINIMUM wage totalling £ 4,000 for each year of this contract. This will be calculated by taking the sum of your earnings between 1st July and 30th June each year.

FOR AND ON BEHALF OF
THE MANCHESTER UNITED FOOTBALL CLUB LTD.

L. Olive   Secretary

Pat Crerand: *My terms and conditions as a Manchester United player in 1966. This two-year contract from July 1966 was to cover the period in which we would win both the Championship and the European Cup - basic wage £65 per week. The letter that came with the contract explained the incentives that were available in a successful season.*

transformation was amazing. West Berlin was a lively, jumping place, full of light, but the East was completely dark, no lights, no advertising, nothing; only the grey walls of the buildings. And the food was terrible. The people there could not get anything – clothes, chocolate, all kinds of things that we took for granted. They would have given you any price you wanted for a bottle of whisky.

It was also the coldest place we have ever played in. Nobody could remember being so cold before. We played the match in a stadium right next to the Wall. Beating them 2-0 helped to warm us up, but probably, as a game, it was more interesting for their spectators to see a visiting team from the Western part of the planet.

As for their style of life, they were welcome to it. East Berlin was like some thriller movie with Humphrey Bogart in it, where the only light came from one bulb hanging on a long flex from the ceiling. The walls were all cracked and

Denis Law: *I always liked to see the captain doing the hard work. Noel Cantwell and I visited the set of* 55 Days in Peking *when we were in Madrid for the European Cup match in 1966.*
Right *Travelling long distances was a long-winded business in 1967. This was the schedule for our flight back from Australia – six stops on the way home.* **Below** *A collection of happy travellers as the team arrives in Malta, one of our favourite places.*

BOAC

Sydney	
	4 hrs. 45 mins.
	Lunch
Perth	
	5 hrs. 15 mins.
	Afternoon Tea
Singapore	
	3 hrs. 55 mins.
	Dinner
Calcutta	
	3 hrs.
	Dinner
	for joining passengers
	Refreshments
Karachi	
	7 hrs. 10 mins.
	Breakfast
Rome	
	1 hr. 50 mins.
	Breakfast
	for joining passengers
	Refreshments
	for transit passengers
Frankfurt	
	1 hr. 20 mins.
	Breakfast
	for joining passengers
	Refreshments
	for transit passengers
London	

For alcoholic drinks and cigarettes
please refer to the Bar Tariff

719 12667

Europa-Pokal 1965/66

MDN 0,30

Jürgen Nöldner

Denis Law

Manchester United (England)

gegen ASK Vorwärts Berlin

17. November 1965 - 14.00 Uhr - Walter-Ulbricht-Stadion

peeling, and it was just before the interrogation scene. No thanks. We were very glad to be away from it.

On the brighter side, we did stay at some nice places and the best of these was Malta. We went there to play Hibernians in the first round of the European Cup in 1967-68.

Malta was amazing. They are all crazy about Manchester United. They even have their own Supporters Club. On the way from the airport a cavalcade of about a hundred cars followed our coach to the Phoenicia Hotel.

The hotel itself was fantastic, and the service was absolutely brilliant. There was nothing the Maltese could not do for us. Having said that, they followed us everywhere. When you went up to your room, there were a dozen blokes already in there. When you went out to the toilet from the restaurant, five or six of them followed you in. Nor was there any possibility of going outside the hotel. We would have been mobbed – in the nicest way, of course, but it is not very relaxing when you have a football match in front of you.

The pitch, mind you, was not in the same class as the hotel. It was terrible. It was made of compressed sand and was extremely bumpy. Whenever the ball went up in the air, it was a lottery what it would do when it landed. To our embarrassment, we never got hold of the game and could only squeeze out a 0-0 draw, which is not what you

expect a British side to do in Malta, who are among the weakest of the competing nations. Luckily, or not so luckily, we had a 4-0 lead in our pockets from the first leg at Old Trafford, and there was nothing to get in a panic about.

We still see our Maltese fans today. They come over on special trips to see a home match at United. They are as crazy about the club as they ever were.

Our trip to play ASK Vorwaerts in East Berlin **(top)** *was a very different experience to playing Hibernian in Malta* **(left)***, but at least we won the game in Berlin.*

We could have won the European Cup three times. In 1965-66 we had our first taste of what we could achieve, only to fall at a hurdle we should have cleared with some ease.

In the early rounds we knocked out HJK Helsinki of Finland and ASK Vorwaerts of East Germany with aggregate scores of 9-2 and 5-1. Then we met Benfica in the third round.

Benfica at that time were one of the top European sides, along with Real Madrid and Inter Milan. In the five seasons between 1960-61 and 1964-65 they had got to the Final four times and won it twice. Everybody of that generation remembers their great

Denis Law: *It looks a bit dark in the Stadium of Light as we toss before the start of the game which turned out to be one of our greatest performances.*

BENFICA
MANCHESTER UNITED
taça dos clubes campeões europeus
às 21.45 h

9 / 3 / 66

George Best is soon on target against Benfica, and 'El Beatle' is born.

players in the Portuguese World Cup side of 1966 – the brilliant Eusebio, Torres the tall man at centre-forward, Simoes on the wing. In fact Benfica supplied more or less the whole of the national side.

We beat them 3-2 at Old Trafford, but we knew that one goal was not going to be enough to see us through. The return leg would be hard work.

We went over to Lisbon. In seven years of European football Benfica had never been defeated at their home ground, the Stadium of Light, and in our last visit to the Portuguese capital we had been thumped 5-0 by Sporting Lisbon in the Cup-Winners' Cup of 1963-64. It was something the Portuguese fans were delighted to remind us of, and on the way to the stadium they surrounded our slow-moving coach and held up five fingers at the windows.

The game started twenty minutes late while Eusebio was presented with his award for European Footballer of the Year. Then, as the rockets went off, we at last got going.

In that match we played our best-ever game as a team. Nothing we did before or after can compare with the way we turned it on that night. We thrashed them 5-1.

George Best had the game won inside 12 minutes with two goals. Later he set up John Connelly for another. He played beautifully. It was the night he changed from being just a football star into a huge celebrity. The Portuguese newspapers called him 'El Beatle' and after that the hype and media attention never let him go. The match was a high point for all of us, but it also meant that life for George would never be the same again. For people who knew what a fantastic player he was, it was inevitable that something like this would happen one day. He had such an amazing talent, it was only a question of time before he faced up to a big match like this one, and took the opposition apart.

In April we met Partizan Belgrade in the first leg of the semi-final. In between this match and our triumph in Lisbon a lot had happened, none of it good for United. Denis had knee trouble, which had already kept him out of the previous Saturday's League match, and Bestie had been hacked down in the first of two FA Cup semi-finals against Preston. He had a cartilage injury and although he started the game against Partizan with the knee strapped up, he broke down and had to have treatment. He limped on but that was his last match of the season.

Denis Law: We should have scored an early goal. George sent over a cross which I only had to tap in from two yards out. I swung and missed, the ball hit my thigh, bobbed up and hit the crossbar and they knocked it away. George also missed one from no distance. Then Partizan scored, their crowd got behind them and they ran out 2-0 winners.

Pat Crerand: In the return match we still thought we could beat them. There was nothing particularly special about them, although they did have a hard defence and gave us little in the way of chances. Nobby Stiles scored after 73 minutes but that was all we could do. Also in the game Nobby punched someone and the referee got him mixed up with me, so I was sent off for it.

It was a massive disappointment. We had done the hard bit, and done it magnificently, beating Benfica in such style. Then we came a cropper against mediocre opponents.

It was two years before we received our next opportunity, in the 1967-68 season. In the intervening year Celtic had become the first British club to win the European Cup, beating Inter Milan 2-1 in the Final in Lisbon.

John Connelly is in the net but the Partizan goalkeeper has the ball.

Pat Crerand: *Years later I came across most of my ticket allocation for the European Cup semi-final against Real Madrid. I had never have got round to handing them out to family or friends. I can't think why no one asked me for any.*

Pat Crerand: *Getting the lowdown on the opposition. Somehow my son Patrick found his way into the Real Madrid dressing-room when they trained at Old Trafford the day before the semi-final.*

Pat Crerand: My mother and my father-in-law, who were both great Celtic fans, went down to Lisbon to see the Final. We, however, were on a summer tour in Hawaii. From there we flew to New Zealand.

We arrived in Auckland at about half-past seven in the morning and as soon as I could I rang the *Auckland Star*. I asked to speak to the Sports Department and I asked the guy there:

'Who won the match last night in the European Cup Final?'

He had no idea what I was talking about, hadn't the faintest clue.

There was a little English girl standing there next to me.

'I was listening to your accent,' she said, 'I hope you don't mind. As far as the game is concerned, I don't know what it was about or who was playing, but whatever it was it was the first time a British side had done it.'

And that is how I knew Celtic had won the European Cup. I was delighted that they had done it but I think I felt a bit jealous too because we could have won it before them.

Later that year they had the 'Sports Personality of the Year' awards on television and I remember Matt Busby presenting the Team of the Year trophy to Jock Stein. They also had the European Cup trophy with them in the studio and Jock said to Matt:

'Well, hopefully I'm presenting this to you next year.'

Once Celtic had won the trophy, it had the effect of making us believe that United could definitely win it too, and

George Best scores our only goal against Real Madrid in the first leg of the European Cup semi-final at Old Trafford

this cleared away a lot of inhibitions and gave us confidence as well.

In the first round of the competition we beat Hibernians of Malta 4-0 on aggregate, even though we failed to score on their ground. We held Sarajevo of Yugoslavia to a 0-0 draw away, then only just beat them 2-1 at Old Trafford.

Gornik Zabrze, the Polish side, were an even tougher proposition. Denis was out with a knee injury but we beat them 2-0 at home and held on to lose only 1-0 in Poland. That game was played in terrible conditions in thick snow. I know it is the same for both sides, but there was so much snow stacked up between the goalposts it made the goals look smaller! Ridiculous though it sounds, this may even have given us a slight advantage as our principal objective on the day was to stop them from scoring.

Next we had a big semi-final against Real Madrid. They were not the great side they had been when they won the European Cup in the first five years of its existence, but neither were we at our strongest. George Best got us a goal and we had to be content with that. A slender 1-0 lead was not much to take to a place like the Bernabeu Stadium in Madrid. Remembering our previous semi-final against Partizan Belgrade, the question nobody wanted to face up to was: 'Had we blown it again?'

Gifts were often exchanged between teams on European occasions. We were all given a gold tie-pin by Real Madrid.

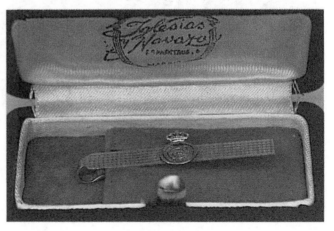

UNITED THE LEGENDARY YEARS

Pat Crerand: *Off to Madrid for the second leg. Whenever we travelled on club business we were always expected to be properly dressed.*

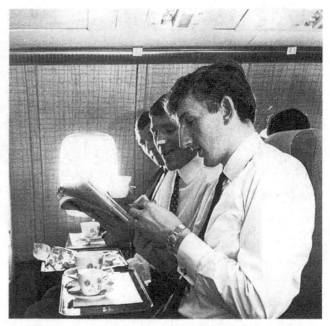

Denis Law: I had failed a fitness test on my knee and watched the game in Madrid from the dugout. At half-time they were leading 3-1 and it looked to be all over. They had an inside forward called Amancio who was having a fantastic game. In fact they could have had an even bigger lead.

I was sitting next to Matt Busby when they started the second half. After about five minutes I was beginning to notice something. I turned to Matt and said:

'It looks to me as if they think they've won it. They've gone back into second gear. I think we've got a chance if we can get a goal back.'

The goal that clinched our place in the European Cup final. Bill Foulkes (in the backgound) sidefoots the ball and Brian Kidd watches as it slips past the Real keeper.

And we did. And then we got another. It was Bill Foulkes who scored the third one, the goal that eventually put us through.

When he scored it, I jumped up in the dugout and punched the air. Except that I didn't punch the air because I smashed my fist into one of the metal poles holding the roof together. I was in agony for a week afterwards. Never mind, I knew now that we had a great chance to win the European Cup.

Pat Crerand: Denis is right. We went out in the second half and after a few minutes I started thinking, 'This team isn't bothered. They think the game is over.'

We started pushing forward, and they let us. I threw the ball in to George and he crossed it. David Sadler appeared from nowhere and turned it into the net.

I remember the deathly silence that followed. I thought for a moment that David had missed it, then the United fans in the crowd went potty. That goal put the two teams level on aggregate, but still Real Madrid sat back and didn't come at us.

So then I thought to myself, 'This team's knackered. They've gone.' Then we scored again through Billy Foulkes, and if we'd had time to go forward again I think we might have got another.

Then it was all over – we were in the Final!

Benfica won their semi-final against Juventus with an impressive aggregate of 3-0, winning both matches. However, in the build-up to the Final I was convinced we

Denis Law: *We were beseiged by fans at our hotel in Madrid after our semi-final win.*

Pat Crerand: *We are on our way to Wembley – a few last words to the press before the train leaves Manchester.*

Above *It was Brian Kidd's 19th birthday.*
Below *Getting the feel of the Wembley turf before lining up for the start of the European Cup final.*

were going to win the European Cup because we had already beaten them twice two years before.

On the morning of the game we went off to Mass. A Christian Brothers' school had put on a special Mass for us and Matt was such a deeply religious man that everybody went – Catholics, Protestants, whatever. Even friends of ours staying at the hotel all joined in.

It was 29 May and Derby Day. Robert Sangster, the racehorse owner, asked us round to a little do at his house in the afternoon. We had met him over in Bermuda the previous year and so now he asked us round to his house.

The last time we had met he said, 'For next year's Derby, put everything you've got on Sir Ivor.'

A few of the lads were into gambling. We watched the race on television that afternoon and Sir Ivor won by a mile, so some of the team were already in profit by tea-time. We went back to the hotel, had a couple of hours in bed, then a light meal and it was time to set off for Wembley.

It was not exactly a home fixture but the streets were packed just like they had been in 1966 for the World Cup Final, and now everybody was supporting Manchester United. No English club had won it yet, and so the crowds were looking to us.

Denis, unfortunately, was in hospital with his knee problem so had to miss the game. Our team that night was:

Stepney; Brennan, Dunne; Crerand, Foulkes, Stiles; Best, Kidd, Charlton, Sadler, Aston.

It was still very warm when I went out on the pitch before the game. It was Brian Kidd's 19th birthday and the crowd sang 'Happy Birthday to You' – a fantastic experience for a young Manchester lad who had only just come into the side.

I thought we had control of the game for most of the first 90 minutes. There were a lot of nerves out there but we were holding them 1-1 when suddenly Eusebio burst through.

Bobby Charlton watches his header fly into the far corner past Benfica's wrong-footed goalkeeper Jose Henrique. We are one up.

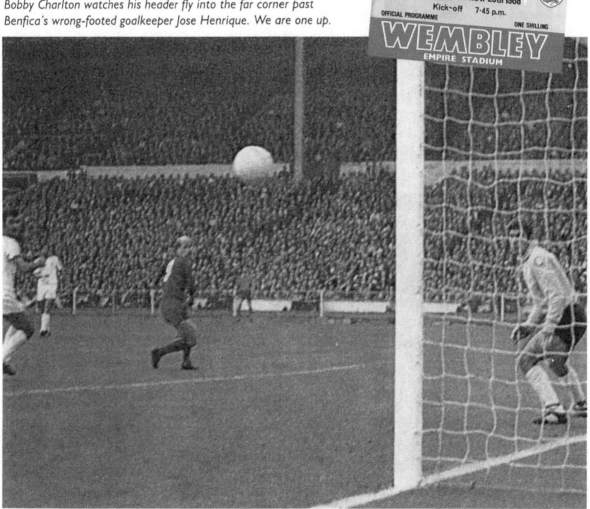

Above *George Best scores early in extra-time and there's no way back for Benfica.*
Below *To many supporters, the greatest moment in United's history as Bobby Charlton raises the European Cup.*

He was clear and he seemed certain to score. All he had to do was sidestep Alex Stepney and thank you very much. Instead he blasted it, and Alex stood up to him and caught the ball.

At the break Matt Busby came on. He was angry.

'You're giving the ball away too much. It's a warm night and it's not a pitch to give the ball away. Get hold of the ball again, don't give it away and start knocking it about amongst yourselves.'

The game restarted and about seven minutes later we were three up. In that spell we played as we really can play. George ran past them from the

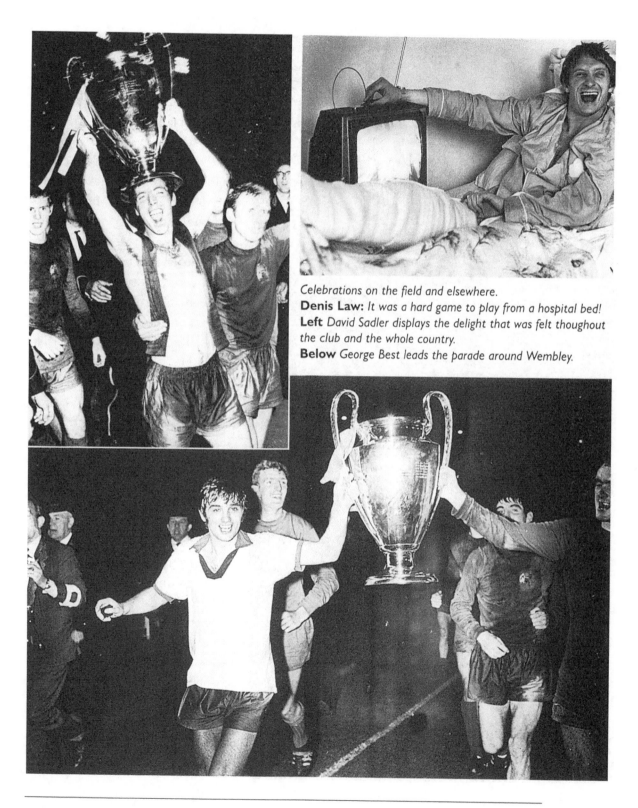

Celebrations on the field and elsewhere.
Denis Law: *It was a hard game to play from a hospital bed!*
Left *David Sadler displays the delight that was felt thoughout the club and the whole country.*
Below *George Best leads the parade around Wembley.*

halfway line for a wonderful goal. Brian Kidd headed the next and then Bobby hit one to give us a 4-1 lead from which we were never going to be pulled back.

All this time Denis was far away in hospital, in a place called St Joseph's which is run by nuns in Moss Side, Manchester. Although he was not exactly alone, he was not where we would have wanted him to be – out there on the pitch with us.

Meanwhile, David Coleman had plans for him. David was doing the TV commentary that night. He is also a local lad, a United supporter and in his time a very keen athlete who used to train at Old Trafford with the Busby Babes side that lost so many people in the Munich crash.

After the game I remember going into the dressing-room with a bottle of champagne and David was there, delighted for us. He was also telling us about Denis.

The nuns had known well enough that he wanted to watch the game, and that he had a few pals coming in that night. So they cleared the two beds on either side of Denis to make room for everybody. The BBC knew this too, and their plan was to go over

Pat Crerand: *Brian Kidd's turn to carry the cup but I've got the ribbons!*

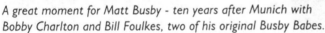

*A great moment for Matt Busby - ten years after Munich with
Bobby Charlton and Bill Foulkes, two of his original Busby Babes.*

to the hospital immediately after the match and for David Coleman to interview Denis.

Denis, however, did not get interviewed because he broke down from the emotion of
the night. I think the McEwans and whatever else had something to do with it too, but
I know he did not appear on TV. If you ask him about it now, he only laughs and says
what a great night it was.

From Wembley the team went on to a banquet at the
Russell Hotel. Joe Loss and his Orchestra played us into the
room with 'Congratulations'. It was a fantastic night, but in
one sense a very sad one. The club had invited not only
representatives of all the teams we had played in the previous
rounds, but also they asked the parents of all the lads who had
died in Munich.

That gave an extra dimension to the evening. I remember
having a long chat with Duncan Edwards's dad. The boys'
parents were all delighted that we had won the European Cup
but the occasion also brought back sad memories as well as
great ones.

It was a long party. I don't think anyone went to bed that
night – except Denis up in Manchester who was in bed already.

Next day we got up very late and went back to Manchester,
where the whole city was out on the streets. We arrived on a

Pat Crerand: *I don't know how
Noreen and I look so bright. This was
the morning after outside our hotel in
Russell Square*

Pat Crerand: *On our way to the Town Hall* **(above)** *and* **(below)** *my turn to say a few words.*

private train and how anyone knew this train was ours, I'll never know. There were people waving to us on all the stations we passed through.

Before we left London I saw an old Scottish guy I knew at Euston Station. He was there with his pal and I said to him, 'Are you going back to Manchester?'

'Yes,' he said, 'we're going back on the train.'

I said, 'You're not getting on that one,' pointing to ours. 'That's a private train.'

They didn't say anything. I got on our train and sat down. A few minutes later I walked through to the bar – and there they were! I stayed and had a laugh with them for a while, but didn't say anything to anyone about them.

In Manchester we had a coach to take us round the town. By the time I had got on board, these two lads were on it too, sitting down and quietly enjoying the view.

We got to the Town Hall for the civic reception. We were received by the Mayor and then the team went out on the balcony to show everyone the European Cup. Well, not just the team – these two lads were there as well, standing next to me. It was unbelievable how they got away with it. Only after you've had a hard night would you even try it on.

Denis Law: A few hours later Matt Busby came round to the hospital and he brought the European Cup with him. That was a great moment for me – and a very special one that I don't think many people either knew about or will remember.

Pat Crerand: Not being in the team for the European Cup Final was very hard on Denis. Even though he's got a winner's medal he is still likely to say, 'Oh, I didn't win the European Cup. I wasn't in the team.' I tell him that's ridiculous. A lot of players appeared in some of the earlier rounds, including him, and they helped us to win the Cup just as much as those who were in the Final. In any case, if he had been fit, there is no question that he would have been selected.

The following year, 1968-69, we entered the European Cup with high hopes. In the early rounds we beat Waterford (agg. 10-2), Anderlecht (4-3) and Rapid Vienna (3-0). Our opponents in the semi-final were AC Milan, who had put out Celtic in the quarter-final with typical low-scoring performances, 0-0 at home and 1-0 away.

The first leg was at San Siro, played before 80,000 fanatics. We were playing reasonably well but then, either side of half-time, they were awarded two very dubious goals, so much so that we began to wonder if there wasn't something more than the other eleven players working against us. We also lost Nobby Stiles, who had to be carried off after his knee suddenly locked up.

In the return game we knew it would be tight because Italian defences, especially in those days, never gave anything away. We had a tremendous battle with them for 70 minutes and then Bobby Charlton pulled one back after a move with George Best.

Pat Crerand: In those last ten minutes we attacked them with all our power. Then I had the ball. I took it to the dead-ball line and knocked it into the middle. There was a scramble of legs as several players went for it. Denis connected and the ball was a good two feet over the line before their full-back, Anquilletti, dived in and hooked it out with his left hand.

The referee, a Frenchman, gave us nothing. He was standing some way back, but his decision was totally unfair and wrong because, if he had done his job properly, he only had two choices. If the ball had gone over the line, he should have given us a goal. If it had not, he should have given us a penalty. To pretend, as he did, that he did not see anything, made us think he had definitely been got at in some way before the match.

Later on, AC Milan did get into trouble with UEFA for tactics that bordered on bribery, offering gifts to referees and linesmen, and so on, which everyone involved must have known was illegal.

Whatever the case for us, we were denied the play-off match which that goal would have earned us, and we were out of the European Cup.

By then Matt Busby had pulled back from the team manager's job and Wilf

McGuinness had recently taken over. Later, in December 1970, Matt was recalled to shore up a deteriorating position at United, but then he only carried on for a further six months. You could say, in fact, that the semi-final matches against AC Milan were the last big event of his long career in charge at Old Trafford.

Although it was not perhaps the best note for him to finish on, he had nevertheless achieved his dream the year before against Benfica. That was something that would live for ever.

Above *A dream fulfilled, but the celebrations* (**left and below**) *went on.*

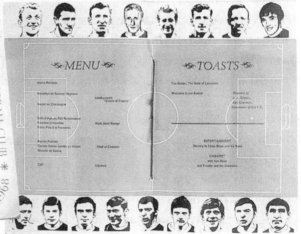

THE WORLD CLUB CHAMPIONSHIP

On paper it looked a terrific fixture – the Champions of Europe against the Champions of South America.

Matt was always a great advocate of looking outwards. We should never be content with playing just in England. Football is a world game and we should be looking to play it all over the world.

When you think of South America, you think first of the great Brazilian teams. You think of playing against Pele or Jairzinho, Rivelino or Tostao at one of their great clubs – Santos, Botafogo, Corinthians or Cruzeiro. We got the Argentinians.

Clubs from the Argentine were winning everything in those years. And no wonder, they kicked everybody else off the field.

Denis Law: *Off to Argentina, little did we know what was in store for us. Brian Kidd, Francis Burns and I compare passport photos at the airport..*

Pat Crerand: I thought it would be a total farce. I had seen Celtic play Racing Club of Argentina the year before at Hampden Park. Celtic beat them 1-0 and they kicked Celtic from pillar to post. They didn't try to play at all.

The day after the game I was in the George Hotel in Buchanan Street with Jock Stein and Neillie Mochan, the Celtic trainer.

I said to them, 'I can't believe you're going over there to play them again. You'll be murdered. You'll have to wear armour-plated suits.'

Sure enough, it was the same again in Argentina – a vicious brawl which Racing Club won, so Celtic had to play a third game in which five players were sent off. It was a complete shambles.

Matt Busby, for all his international outlook, also had his doubts, but the arrangements were in place and off we had to go, to play Estudiantes.

Two years earlier, of course, England had beaten Argentina in the quarter-finals of the World Cup. That had been a rough match and afterwards Alf Ramsey, the England manager, had called them animals and ran on the field to stop his players exchanging jerseys with them.

Nobby Stiles had been in the England side and he was not a popular man in Argentina. They labelled him 'The Assassin' and we had to have permanent police protection. We went to church there on the Sunday night and there were guys from the police sitting in the church holding sten guns.

Those were the rules of the game over there and so, for all our time in Buenos Aires, there was no chance to get out and have a look round – we'd never have come back alive.

When we arrived, they put us out to stay at the Hindu Club, a big place outside the city. We were on the sixteenth floor of a huge apartment block, and the lifts did not work. Every time we went out, we had to trail down 32 flights of stairs and 32 back up again. If you realised, halfway down, that you had left something behind in your room, you certainly didn't go back for it. The lifts were out of order all the time we were there – until the match was over. Then they came back into service.

That was the start of the battle. Then, because of the bad feeling in the Celtic games the previous year, it was decided that the two teams should meet before the match. It was an hour and a half bus ride each way, something which, the night before the match, nobody really fancied doing.

We were shown into a big room full of people drinking and smoking. The other team had not arrived so we waited for them. We hung about at this reception for two hours but they never showed up. So then Matt, who was furious at the way we had been treated, took us back to the Hindu Club again.

The only friendly exchange was before the game began.

To be fair, the Argentinians were not the only people to try and get one up on us before a game. We had the same trouble going over to Milan. Before the match we stayed in Brescia, which is about an hour away, and the whole of the night their fans were driving round the building, tooting their horns and blowing trumpets and doing anything they could to put us off and stop us from sleeping.

Above *Another atrocious tackle, this time on Willie Morgan. The armed guards in the background should have come onto the field to arrest this Argentinian player.* **Right** *Five months after the joy of Wembley, David Sadler again sums up the mood of the Manchester United contingent, and gets some words of consolation from Wilf McGuinness.*

Facing page Pat Crerand: *An Estudiantes shirt was at least something to come away with.*

THE WORLD CLUB CHAMPIONSHIP

Denis Law: Because of the trouble in England in the World Cup, the Argentinians assumed that everyone in the United team was English. The fact that we were a mixture of English, Scots and Irish meant nothing to them.

It was one of those games where I wished the referee had blown for full-time after about ten minutes. There was no way we were going to be allowed to play any kind of football. Whenever we went near anybody, they fell on the ground and shrieked for a foul. When they fouled us, the referee played on. It was a nightmare.

Pat Crerand: I remember the feller going over the top to Bobby Charlton. The blood was spurting out of Bobby's leg and he had to have stitches in the wound. The guy who did it was a doctor, Bilardo, who later became manager of the Argentinian national side.

There was a lot of blood that night. In the 14th minute someone head-butted Nobby Stiles and immediately fell to the ground to suggest it was Nobby who had done it to him. The referee seemed to fall for it and was going to send Nobby off until he got closer and saw the cut which had opened up over his eye. Nobby struggled on through the match, getting kicked, punched and spat on like the rest of us, until the linesman on his side of the field ignored a blatant offside by Estudiantes. Nobby's patience gave out. He flashed the linesman a V-sign and this time the referee did send him off.

Another trick they had, after they had knocked you over, was to rush in and help you up again. From a distance it looked all very sporting but in actual fact while they pulled you to your feet they were busy pinching the tender skin under your armpits. If you have ever had it done to you, you will know it hurts like hell.

Eventually we got beaten 1-0. Three weeks later the English newspapers were not taking many risks when they looked forward to the 'Battle of Old Trafford'. They were right, it was exactly the same as it had been in Buenos Aires.

Denis Law: They got an early goal and that set us back on our heels. After about twenty minutes I had to be carried off after their goalkeeper dived at me with his studs up and raked a big gash down my right shin.

Later in the match George Best got in a scuffle with one of their players, Medina, and both were sent off. The press pictures of the incident always show the shot of Medina being led off the field in the arms of two of their team officials. The player himself is doubled up with grief and has a hand over his face. He probably burst into tears as well.

Left *Jose Medina is sent off at Old Trafford but George Best had to go as well.*

UNITED THE LEGENDARY YEARS

So then we were down to ten men each. Late in the game Willie Morgan converted a free-kick from Pat, and that brought the scores level for the night, though we were still 1-2 down on aggregate. Then, on the stroke of time, Brian Kidd smashed in a cross only to find that the referee had already finished blowing his whistle and the game was over.

We had lost. Estudiantes could call themselves World Club Champions, but it was difficult to care either way. After the fiasco of those two terrible matches, we had all had enough of the Argentinians.

The following year Estudiantes played AC Milan, who had gone on to beat Ajax 4-0 in the Final of the European Cup. Milan actually beat the Argentinians 4-2 on aggregate, though both matches were blood-baths, as usual. Afterwards Lodetti, the Milan midfield player, said the way Estudiantes played was 'a permanent crime against the spirit of football'.

The writing was on the wall for this very dubious fixture. In 1977, after Liverpool had won the European Cup, they were invited to take part in a similar tournament. They politely said no thank you.

EUROPEAN SOUTH AMERICAN CUP 1968
No. 9

KICK-OFF 7:45 p.m.

MANCHESTER UNITED OF ENGLAND VERSUS ESTUDIANTES OF ARGENTINA OCTOBER 16 1968

price 1/-

UNITED REVIEW

THE OFFICIAL PROGRAMME OF MANCHESTER UNITED FOOTBALL CLUB

16 October 1968 – a sad night for football.

We have seen how Matt Busby worked to create a family atmosphere at Old Trafford, and how this produced a team spirit that ran through the whole club. Here we look a little more closely at the man, his beliefs and how he set about the job of making United the most successful British club of the 1960s.

He was a deeply religious man. He was a regular churchgoer and he never used bad language or resorted to crude expressions when he was angry. It may not be a particularly good thing to get angry, but there were a few times when he got very angry. He had his own strong views about certain things, and one of them was gambling.

Pat Crerand: Footballers are well known for playing cards to pass the time on trains and coach journeys. One time there was a group of United people going down to Wembley to see the match between England and the Rest of the World (Denis was playing for them). A few of the lads were playing cards for money.

Matt never liked this. In a club like ours, he thought it could go wrong and spoil relationships between players. Someone might get upset or even violent, or lose money he could not afford to lose, or have trouble paying someone what he owed. All those things could lead to lasting trouble.

So Matt walked into this compartment where the lads were having their game. He picked the money up off the table and threw it out the train window. Imagine! A Scottish man throwing money out the window. Anyway, it had its effect. They never played cards for money again, at least not when Matt was anywhere near.

Denis Law: It was 1966. I had a couple of children and another was

Denis Law: *Read on over the page for the full story behind this newspaper cutting.*

MR. SMITH, alias Denis Law, came to town yesterday to make his peace with Manchester United. Law was listed as Mr. Smith on his flight from Aberdeen.

The visit was a closely guarded secret—so much so that even Matt Busby, United's manager, was surprised by Law's arrival at Old Trafford.

But I accompanied him on the plane.

Law, whose ultimatum for a five-figure re-signing fee was answered by Busby placing him on the transfer list last week, told me during the flight :—

"It has been a hectic week . . . one I will never forget . . . a nightmare.

A clanger

"I made my demand on the spur of the moment. When I drop a clanger it has to be a big one."

At Manchester Airport he was met by Players' Union secretary Cliff Lloyd, who had

By JIM PARKINSON

urged him to settle his differences with the club.

At Old Trafford there was a 40-minute talk which ended with Law asking to be taken off the transfer list and signing a new two-year contract WITHOUT a fee.

Then the £115,000 player admitted :—

"I have been foolish. I should have sought professional advice before doing anything so rash. I am very sorry. I never really wanted to leave United and I would hope now to finish my playing days with the club."

Busby commented : "It took courage for Denis to come to admit he was wrong. Only big men do such things."

Last night Law flew back to Aberdeen, where his wife Diana is expecting their second child.

Mr. Smith was much happier on the return trip.

on the way. A few quid extra would be very useful, so I thought I'd try it on with the manager.

I wrote him a letter telling him the terms I wanted, and what would happen if he did not agree to them. I did not give him the letter – I was too scared to go in and face him directly, so I left it with the assistant secretary.

A couple of days later I was up in Scotland playing golf. Suddenly a newspaper reporter came running across the course to our group. He had a message for me – 'You're on the transfer list!'

Denis Law: *This was the public handshake in the shadow of Old Trafford at the end of a traumatic period. I was glad it was all over.*

Matt had made no attempt to communicate with me, he just put me straight on the transfer list. It was big news for the sports pages, and the club and I received a whole lot of publicity we could have done without. Soon after that I had a call from Jane Busby, Matt's wife (or Lady Jane, as we later called her).

'What are you doing?' she asked in a steely voice.

That was it. I couldn't fight her as well. I had to fly down from Aberdeen to sort it out with him.

I went to see Matt in his office. Outside the ground all the press guys were watching and making up their stories – there he goes to apologise to the boss, that kind of thing.

I went into his office. He handed me a letter which he had already written and had typed out. It was from me. It said, 'I am very sorry to have embarrassed Manchester United ... for whatever reason ... no man is bigger than the club, etc, etc.'

I thought to myself, 'That's lovely. We haven't even talked about it and he's got the whole thing written out.'

So then I had to sign the letter and go out to the media guys and say how sorry I was. The affair was then quickly forgotten. However, the only thing that nobody ever found out was that I did get my rise. As far as the public was concerned, I didn't get anything. I was quite happy with that part of it, although it was a traumatic experience at the time.

Pat Crerand: I can add something to that story. While Denis was up in Scotland, Matt came to see me in hospital where I was having something done to my nose to help me breathe more easily.

I said to him, 'Boss, he's such an important player for Manchester United, you've got to keep him at the club ...'

Matt was quite irate at the time and he said, 'I shall certainly keep Denis – if he does what I tell him to do.'

Although Matt always knew his own mind about the important things, just once or twice you could expect to hold your own with him. There was a certain pub in Manchester called the Brown Bull which some of the United players made quite famous during the Sixties. In fact it was there that I went after our victory in the European Cup. After all the formalities of the post-match banquet and the civic reception the next day it was good just to slip down there and unwind with some of your mates – people who knew the game and who you felt at home with.

Matt, bless him, could never get the name of this pub right. One day it was the 'Brown Cow', next time it was the 'Black Bull'.

If he ever challenged you with something like 'Were you down there in the Brown Cow?' you had an instant answer.

'What, me, boss? No, never.'

It was a perfect solution. He never got to the bottom of whatever he was probing into, which probably was not important anyway. And you never had to say anything that was not the truth.

When it came to dealing with Bestie, Matt was not so sure of himself. After his brilliant start at United, followed by the 'El Beatle' period when he was probably the most photographed footballer in the world, George went through a wild period. He started pulling himself out of matches, went missing for days and generally gave the club a hard time.

When things were at their worst with Bestie, Matt had already stepped down as team manager. Of all the people at the club, however, he was still the most likely person to be able to deal with George. Don't forget, he had signed him up as a kid, had

DAILY EXPRESS

NOT TO BE SOLD SEPARATELY

BACK BRITAIN · BUY BRITISH

MANCHESTER DERBY MATCH

COLOUR SPECIAL

Pictures by
GEORGE BIRCH
JAMES DAKIN
JOE DARBY

United aim for a double
City plan quick revenge

MARCH OF THE MODS

By
JAMES LAWTON

THEY walk self-confidently, and well-heeled, through the heart of a great city . . . two young men with a world at their fashionable feet, an empire at hand.

Their world is the ever-widening frontiers of club and international Soccer, their city is Manchester, and the names, of course, are George Best and Mike Summerbee.

Both mean the same things to the supporters of United and the boldly resurgent City . . . dazzling skills, at times staggering courage, and perhaps most warming of all is the aura of permanence about their union with the Soccer crime of Manchester.

"It's hard to explain really," says Summerbee, "how you can get so fond of a place so quickly. It's as if I am part of the city; and it is a wonderfully alive city, a place where it all seems to be happening. And it is . . . for me at least!"

FLAMBOYANT

Summerbee, as warm and as friendly off the field as he is arrogant, flamboyant, and egotistically witty on it, has surged forward these last six months. But he rejects the suggestion that he and Best have formed a "success-set" club with a membership of two.

"I'm a great friend of George's, but there is no question of an 'in-set'. He goes his way and I go mine. He has his style of dress and I have mine. Nobody's copying anyone."

What they do, indisputably, have in common is the easy power to set the mood of half a city.

"I think it would really hurt me to leave Manchester, now," says Mike. Best echoes: "All sorts of people went out of their way to make me feel at home, and in the early days it made all the difference. I just can't imagine leaving Old Trafford now."

Nor, certainly, could Manchester, poised ready for a dramatic display of Soccer power, imagine losing the magnetism of a Best or a Summerbee.

They are clearly servants of the city. But servants who ride in the Lord Mayor's coach!

Manchester's men about Soccer on opposite sides of the city, but side by side as men about town . . . George Best and his leisure-time friend, Mike Summerbee.

Into action ... the idols of a swinging Soccer city

FRANCIS LEE . . . blond bomber, winging to great heights.

NEIL YOUNG . . . unpredictable menace, especially around goal.

TONY COLEMAN . . . watch his left foot and beware his crosses.

DENIS LAW . . . whisper a chance he will take it; give an inch and he will snatch the match.

GEORGE BEST . . . on the field slickness equals off field elegance; no side can plan against him.

Left *George Best and Mike Summerbee led Manchester football into the Swinging Sixties.* **Right** *Happy together – Matt Busby, Manager of the Year in 1968 and George Best, Player of the Year.*

brought him over from Belfast and had looked after his career ever since.

The trouble was, Matt felt more sure of himself with family people, with players who were married and settled in long-term fixed relationships. George did not live like that. Instead of a wife and family he had a succession of girlfriends – dolly birds, models, Miss World candidates, you name it. And although he had bought himself a big house, out in Bramhall, he did not spend a lot of time in it, so there was really nowhere that Matt could go and visit him for the kind of chat he liked to have with players, that is, on their own home ground, surrounded by the usual comforts of a steady existence.

If they had managed to have a chat like that, maybe things would have got sorted out before they went really out of control, as eventually happened.

Then again, had Matt been younger, or in better health, he might have dealt with George with the same energy and decisiveness as he had brought to bear on the case of D Law and the salary demand. As it was, everything was allowed to slip and slide until the final crunch came in December 1972, when Frank O'Farrell was sacked as manager and George was placed on the transfer list. The club then announced that he would never again play for United. George put out a similar announcement, saying that he was giving up football. Neither thing turned out to be lastingly true as he later made a brief comeback. However, it was effectively the end of George's time at United.

People still seem to think that George only had a very brief career, that he came out of nowhere like a rocket and burned himself out in a couple of years. That is completely untrue. George made as many first-team appearances as almost any professional footballer could expect to make – 466 in all, in which time he scored 178 goals, was the club's highest scorer in 1968 and scored more than 20 goals a season five times. The only difference with George was that he became a First Division regular at the age of 17 and packed in his serious football by the time he was 27.

Matt Busby – the man in charge.
Right A thoughful word with Noel Cantwell, the captain who brought him the FA Cup in 1963 and the Championship in 1964-65. **Below** Another Championship in 1966-67.

Facing page
Above Still a tracksuit manager in 1969.
Below A meeting of three great managerial minds, two of them knighted for their contribution to the game - Sir Alf Ramsey, Joe Mercer and Sir Matt Busby.

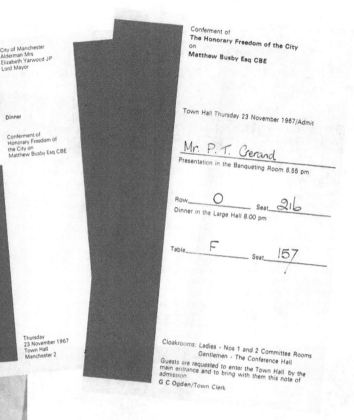

City of Manchester
Alderman Mrs
Elizabeth Yarwood JP
Lord Mayor

Dinner

Conferment of
Honorary Freedom of
the City on
Matthew Busby Esq CBE

Thursday
23 November 1967
Town Hall
Manchester 2

Conferment of
The Honorary Freedom of the City
on
Matthew Busby Esq CBE

Town Hall Thursday 23 November 1967/Admit

Mr. P. T. Crerand

Presentation in the Banqueting Room 6.55 pm

Row _____O_____   Seat ___216___
Dinner in the Large Hall 8.00 pm

Table _____F_____   Seat ___157___

Cloakrooms: Ladies - Nos 1 and 2 Committee Rooms
Gentlemen - The Conference Hall
Guests are requested to enter the Town Hall by the
main entrance and to bring with them this note of
admission
G C Ogden/Town Clerk

Pat Crerand: *Matt Busby was given the Freedom of the City of Manchester in November 1967. Denis and I were among those invited to attend the ceremony, and a banquet afterwards, at the Town Hall.*

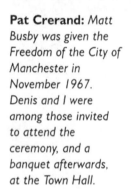

In our finest period, the great six years that began after we won the FA Cup in 1963, George Best was a phenomenal player. And the man who made him was Matt Busby. That too is something that should not be forgotten.

Throughout his whole career at Old Trafford, from the time he took over as manager in 1945 to the time he retired to the board of directors in the early 1970s, Matt commanded tremendous respect from all his players. They all loved him. In some clubs you may find that half the players like the manager and half do not, but everybody at United thought that Matt was special.

The main reason was that he was fair and honest. You knew exactly where you stood with him. There was never an in-between with him, it was all straight down the line. He was a lovely man.

After we had won the European Cup there was a general feeling among the players that Matt wanted to retire. Six weeks after our victory against Benfica he was knighted by the Queen for his services to football and, in particular, to Manchester United.

He had been manager for 23 years and his record was magnificent. He had built three great teams – the Forties side, the Busby babes and our Sixties team which had six great years between 1963 and 1969. Together Sir Matt's teams had won the League Championship five times, the FA Cup twice and now the European Cup.

His health, too, was not what it had been. In the aftermath of Munich, ten years earlier, he was unwell for a long time before his strength came back and he was able to take over fully again from Jimmy Murphy, who had been looking after things since the accident.

Towards the end of the Sixties he was beginning to tire more easily – he was around 60 years old at that time – and he may have thought he had achieved all he could. Our present side would not go on much longer, and maybe the prospect of having to start again and build a fresh side for the next decade was too much for him.

All right, sooner or later Matt would be going. But who would replace him? All kinds of people were being mentioned, including Don Revie and Jock Stein.

Pat Crerand: One day I was in Matt Busby's office and he started talking to me about Jock Stein.

I said to him, 'You know, boss, the

Left The Manchester Evening News *celebrates Matt Busby's knighthood in the 1968 Birthday Honours.*
Right *Jock Stein, who changed his mind about coming to Manchester, but later regretted that decision.*

funny thing about Celtic is that they never give their managers a contract.'

This was something I remembered from my playing time up there. So Matt made a few inquiries, found out that Jock did not have a contract and came back to me. I was going up to Glasgow shortly, where Celtic were playing Ajax in the fourth round of the European Cup.

'Go and speak to Jock,' Matt said. 'See what he thinks about it.'

After the game I went up to Jock's house just behind Hampden Park. Bob Shankly, Bill's brother, was in the house and a couple of other family friends. Jock's kids were there as well. His son George, who was still at school, had just gone to bed. It was about 10.30 at night.

I had known George for a long time and I went up to have a word with him. You wouldn't believe it but this lad, whose father was the manager of Celtic, went to bed with a red No.10 jersey on. He idolised Denis. I also knew that George had just applied to Manchester University and been accepted, which, together with the possibility of Jock coming to Manchester, was an amazing coincidence on its own.

I said to him, 'George, the reason I've come up to Glasgow is because Matt Busby wants your dad to be manager of Manchester United.'

When he got over his surprise, George was all for it. 'That's great,' he said. 'I can't believe it.'

They were all Celtic supporters in the family, of course, but Manchester United was their other great love. Then Jock's daughter came in. I spoke to her about it and she was thrilled to bits.

By this time I had been up the stairs with the kids for a long time, and so Jock came up to see what was happening.

I told him why I had come and Jock just stood there and looked at me, dumbfounded.

I went on, 'Matt wants you to go down and see him and Louis Edwards at Louis' house. If you like, I'll tell Matt we've spoken about it and you can organise it with him.'

Then I remember Jean Stein, Jock's wife, coming up the stairs. She was angry because we had been up there for ages and there were other people in the house.

She said to Jock, 'What are you doing up here? It's the height of bad manners.'

So then I told Jean that Matt wanted Jock to be manager of Manchester United. She thought about it for a few moments, and I could see that she didn't like the idea. Her first reaction was to say things like, 'No, I like Celtic.'

I left it at that. It was hardly for me to get involved in trying to persuade someone that United was a bigger club, the job carried more responsibility and more pay, and all of that. Eventually Jock did go and meet Matt. They had a secret meeting somewhere between Leeds and Liverpool and shook hands on it. As I understood it, Jock had agreed and was going to come.

About ten days later, we were going down to London for a match. Matt came up to me and said, 'Your friend is not a very nice person.'

I said, 'What do you mean?'

He told me about meeting Jock and how they had shaken hands on the deal. Then Matt said, 'I got a message yesterday. He's not coming.'

I said, 'Well, I'm totally amazed.'

Although I knew Jean Stein had had her reservations when I went up to Glasgow, I really thought Jock would have talked her into wanting to come, especially as he had then come down to meet Matt and talk about the job.

Matt, on the other hand, had another idea about why Jock had turned United down. He thought Jock had been using the offer as a way of levering up his wages at Celtic Park. The thought of that had made him angry, and rightly so – if it were true. On the other hand, I knew Jock would not have done that. It was because of his wife that he never came to United. Afterwards he regretted it to the day he died.

It was a surprise to all of the players when Wilf McGuinness was given the job. At the age of 31 he became the youngest manager in the First Division. Not only was there surprise, several of the players had doubts about him.

Wilf's commitment to United was beyond question. The club had been his life. He was a Manchester lad and had joined on the same day as Bobby Charlton. He rose up through the Youth team to the First Division side and made his début in 1955. He won two full England caps at wing-half and still had more or less a full playing career ahead of him when he broke a leg in a match at the end of 1959. He was finished as a player at the age of 22.

Wilf McGuinness coaches the United youngsters in 1967; he was to be given greater responsibilty two years later, when Sir Matt decided to step down.

After that he took over as manager of the Youth team and in 1966 was called up by Alf Ramsey to help with the training of the World Cup side. When he was chosen in April 1969 to take over from Matt he in fact took the job of first-team coach while Matt moved up to general manager. Then in August 1970 he was promoted to full manager and Matt joined the directors.

Some of the players may have had doubts because they had actually played with Wilf

A farewell salute to the Old Trafford crowd from Sir Matt after United's game against Leicester in May 1969 which was supposed to be his last as manager.

in the first team before his accident. This must have made it more difficult for him too. Possibly, if he had come in five or six years later, things would have been different. To be fair, in the short time he was in charge of the team he did an effective job. We got to three semi-finals, two in the League Cup and one in the FA Cup. Then he was sacked, in fact demoted to manager of the reserves.

We talk to Wilf now and he also says that maybe he had been a bit young for the job. It was always going to be a tough one, because people went on thinking we could and should win everything. We were still a good team but we were not the great team of two years before.

It was said that we were getting too old, but that was not altogether true. There were a few players who were getting a bit senior – Bobby Charlton, ourselves and Billy Foulkes – though in fact nobody was any great age. In 1969 Bobby was 32, we were 29 and Billy was 27.

So far as we were concerned, United went from being a major force in Europe to something of a has-been side on the strength of one referee's decision. That was the goal the Frenchman did not give us in the second leg of the European Cup semi-final against AC Milan. We had no doubt that we would have got to the Final if that goal had been allowed to

Above right *Manchester had two clubs to be proud of at the beginning of the 1968-69 season. United as champions of Europe and City as League champions were both in the European Cup.*

Denis Law: *This painting (right) is one of a limited edition of prints celebrating the only time that three European Footballers of the Year played in the same club side. For the benefit of collectors, there are only 300 copies of this print and I have added my signature to those of Messrs Best and Charlton on 100 of them.*

stand. Milan were exhausted by that stage of the game, and in the Final we would have beaten Ajax who were still an up-and-coming side. Then we would still have been in Europe the following year, 1969-70.

Unfortunately, none of that happened. Wilf took charge of the team and after that we only ever achieved minor things. Some clubs may have been content with that, but not United. In the League we sank back to mid-table and in all honesty were getting nowhere.

Above *Sir Matt, as he now was, watches as training breaks up in the grounds of our hotel in Milan before our semi-final first leg.*
Below *It had to be over the line but the referee said no and we were out of the 1969 European Cup.*

After Wilf McGuinness, Sir Matt came back for a few months and then Frank O'Farrell took over as manager. It was a difficult job for him too, of course, but he did well at first and by Christmas 1971 we were top of the League. However, we could not keep it going and soon Frank O'Farrell was on his way, to be succeeded by Tommy Docherty.

Denis Law: It was a very restless period for United. New managers were trying to make us play in ways that were alien to us. After Matt stopped being team manager, in came the 'method' men with their blackboards and hours of tactical lecturing. I hated all that and longed for the old days of Matt saying, 'Just go out there and play. Show them what you can do.'

There was no going back, of course, and a time came when I

Goodbye again. Matt Busby hands over the reins again at the end of the 1970-71 season.

felt I should move on. Johnny Hart, who was then in charge at Manchester City, asked me to go back to Maine Road. Despite continuing knee problems I still felt I had another season left in me, so I agreed to go. By the beginning of the 1973-74 season I was a City player.

Neither of the Manchester clubs had a good year, and by April things were looking serious. City escaped relegation by beating West Ham 2-1 in their last-but-one match of the season. Our last match, incredibly, was against United who were still facing the drop.

After eleven years at Old Trafford I had serious doubts about playing in such a key match, and an emotional local derby on top of that. Tony Book had taken over as City manager and it was he who persuaded me to play.

With eight minutes to go it was 0-0. A ball came over into the box and I just back-heeled it. I did not have a clue where the goal was. It went like an arrow past Alex Stepney and into the net. A couple of minutes later, with Old Trafford still numb from the shock, I was substituted. Soon after that the crowd boiled over and invaded the

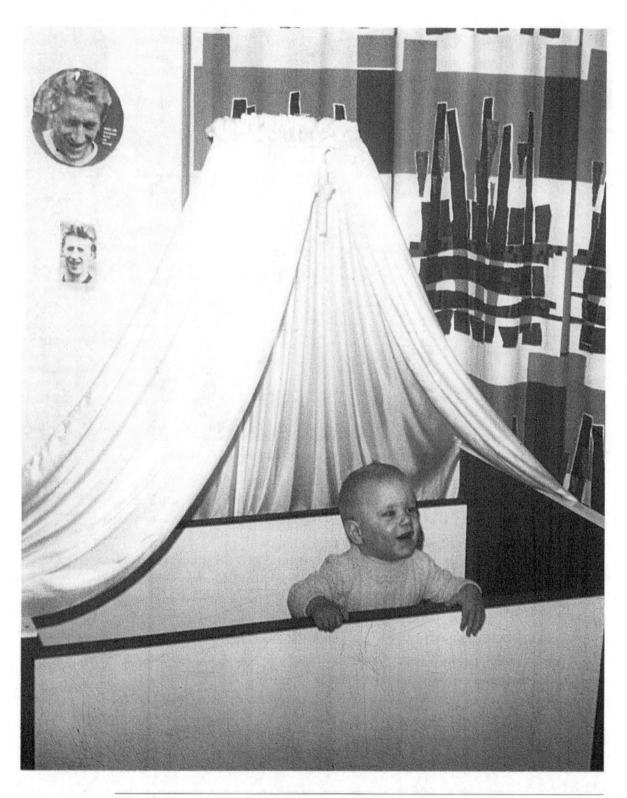

pitch. The referee took all the players off the field and abandoned the match. Later the FA ruled that the result should stand. Manchester United were relegated, and that back-heeled goal was the last time I touched a ball in League football.

The press always liked to claim that it was my goal which sent United down to the Second Division. That is not strictly true because the other two relegation candidates, Birmingham City and Southampton, were both winning their matches when it happened and United would have gone down anyway. All the same, after so many great years at United, I felt very sad at having contributed to the club's miserable end to the season. It was one of the worst weekends of my whole career, as well as being my last in League football.

Denis Law: *My last game in Manchester United colours was against Norwich in 1973 but, of course, my very last appearance was in the No. 10 shirt for Manchester City at Old Trafford in 1974.*

Left *Dennis Bergkamp, the Dutch international, was born soon after our European success and, as I found out only recently, was named after me. His father was a staunch United supporter and this is a photo that I was sent of Dennis B in his cot with photos of me on the wall. An excellent choice of name but either Dennis's dad or the Dutch authorities got the spelling wrong and gave him two 'n's.*

from **Dr. Eric Batley** 11 St. John Street Manchester 3 BLA 4175

January 30th 1968

Dear Mr Glass,

Thank you for sending me your patient Mr Dennis Law.

Two views of the right knee an A.P. and a lateral have been taken and the films are enclosed. These show slight lipping in the outer borders of the lower femur and upper tibia. There is also a small loose body anteriorly and a little spiking in the tibial spines. There is also some lipping in the upper border of the patella. The outer compartment of the joint is very slightly narrowed but the medial compartment appears to be normal.

With kind regards,
Yours sincerely,

Copy to Mr Dalton.

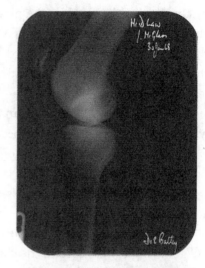

MR. ALAN GLASS.

5 OLD HALL ROAD
RESIDENCE
BROUGHTON PARK.
SALFORD 7
TEL. CHEETHAM HILL 1201.

20, ST JOHN STREET,

MANCHESTER, 3.

TEL. BLACKFRIARS
1010.

21st May 1968.

Dear Dr. McHugh,

Re: Dennis Law.

I saw this player again today. He actually rang me up himself, but I spoke to Mr. Busby and he knows in fact that Dennis has come to see me.

The position is that Dennis tells me that his knee has in fact improved since I saw him last. He is able to train but he still feels the pain on the lateral posterior aspects of the knee and just behind the head of the fibula, when he kicks in a certain position, namely with the leg externally rotated.

When I examined him I found no localised tenderness at the time of todays examination. His range of movement is, as you know, restricted in both flexion and extension but it is certainly no worse than it was. There is no fluid in the knee today and there is no hitch or click. I take the view that if this state of affairs is allowed to carry on in the knee without exploration that it is extremely likely that the knee joint will continue to let him down and in fact it will ruin his footballing career. If on the other hand he submits himself to an exploratory operation, it is from his point of view a run to nothing, because if there is a tag of cartilage and I can remove it successfully which I think is perfectly feasible surgically then he is in with quite a reasonable chance of carrying on to the end of his normal playing time. I have explained this very carefully to Dennis, and in fact I am taking the liberty of dictating the letter in front of him so that he is absolutely fully in the picture. The ball is now of course in the court of the player and the club. I will gladly explore the knee and do my best for him if it is considered my decision is the correct one.

Yours sincerely,

Dr. McHugh.

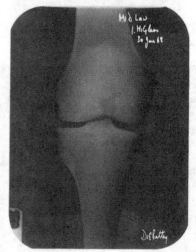

Denis Law: *My knees had been a problem throughout my playing career. The top letter and the X-rays are from January 1968 and things finally came to a head in May with the specialist advice that led to my watching the European Cup Final from a hospital bed.*

Denis Law: *Keeping the knee in working order. We were in Sardinia for pre-season training and boxer Alan Rudkin joined Alex Stepney and myself for this jog along the beach.*

Pat Crerand: The last game I ever played for United was at Blackpool. We drew 1-1 and I got sent off.

What a great way to bow out! It was not my intention at the time to stop playing, but in the period between me getting sent off and the start of the next season, Frank O'Farrell came in as manager.

I missed the start of the season through suspension. The team were playing well, and this lasted until Christmas. So Frank O'Farrell suggested I get involved with the Youth team at Old Trafford. I decided to take the offer and that was the end for me as a United player.

Looking back on the relegation, it turned out to be a blessing. By then three clubs could be promoted and there was no chance that United,

Pat Crerand: *Watching the youth team at Oldham with Tommy Docherty.*

Saturday, 1st May, 1971

BLACKPOOL FOOTBALL CLUB

versus
Manchester Utd.

KICK-OFF 3.00 p.m.

OFFICIAL PROGRAMME

ONE SHILLING
(5 new pence)

MANCHESTER CITY

NEWS 5p

VERSUS
MANCHESTER UNITED
LEAGUE DIVISION ONE
WEDNESDAY
5th MAY 1971
Kick-off 7-45 p.m.

THE AGONY of goalkeeper Ron Healey after he dropped the ball into the net to give Chelsea victory in that second leg battle.
Picture: Daily Express

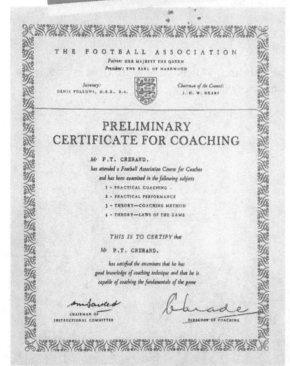

THE FOOTBALL ASSOCIATION

Patron: HER MAJESTY THE QUEEN
President: THE EARL OF HAREWOOD

Secretary:
DENIS FOLLOWS, M.B.E., B.A.

Chairman of the Council:
J. H. W. MEARS

PRELIMINARY CERTIFICATE FOR COACHING

Mr P.T. CRERAND.

has attended a Football Association Course for Coaches and has been examined in the following subjects

1 – PRACTICAL COACHING
2 – PRACTICAL PERFORMANCE
3 – THEORY–COACHING METHOD
4 – THEORY–LAWS OF THE GAME

THIS IS TO CERTIFY that

Mr P.T. CRERAND.

has satisfied the examiners that he has good knowledge of coaching technique and that he is capable of coaching the fundamentals of the game

CHAIRMAN OF INSTRUCTIONAL COMMITTEE

DIRECTOR OF COACHING

Pat Crerand: *My memory is of my last game being the one at Blackpool in which I was sent off, but apparently the records show that my final appearance was at Maine Road the following week. Well, it was almost thirty years ago!* **Left** *First qualifications for a new role.*

with the players they had, would hang about for long in the Second Division.

One season was all they needed. It gave them the chance to reorganise, rebuild and come back again. They finished as Champions and next year were back at the top, even challenging for the double. They finished third in the League and were surprisingly defeated 1-0 in the Cup Final by Southampton, who were then in the Second Division.

This was the start of a new era for Manchester United. Ours was over. For us, though, it had been a fantastic time to play for a truly great club.

Pat Crerand: Denis was one of the great players. He was also easy to play with. He had great pace, vision and awareness of what was around him. He had a fierce shot, whatever he may tell you about it, and he was a great header of the ball, able to hang in the air like a hawk.

A game of header tennis during our early years together at Old Trafford.

It was easy for me to reach him, wherever he was on the field. Sometimes he took a bit of finding because he liked to wander off out of position, first out to one wing and then away to the other. Really, you could say that it was me that made him famous. Without me to send him the ball he would not have been anything. He may not agree with that, of course.

Denis Law: To be fair, what they used to say around that time in Manchester was that if Pat Crerand played well, then Manchester United played well.

He was not, of course, the quickest mover. I used to say that he was a great help to television because they did not need the slow-motion replay when he had the ball.

I played at inside forward. Today I suppose I would be a striker. I used to see Pat with the ball and I would drift out to a fairly wide position on the left. If I then raised my hand he would send over a forty- or fifty-yard ball and I could rely on it landing at my feet or in front of me so I could run on to it.

He was one of the great passers of the ball – not only the long through-passes but also the delicate chips and flicks, the kind of ball that turned defenders and had people mystified until suddenly it was at the feet of one of our front men – Bestie or Bobby or David Herd – and next thing it would be in the back of the net.

It must say something about the spirit which held our Sixties team together, because almost all of us are still living in the Manchester area. The only ones to have moved away are George Best, Jimmy Rimmer, the reserve goalkeeper, who is living in Wales, and Shay Brennan who is in Waterford in Ireland, where he runs a haulage business.

As for the rest of us, Alex Stepney is the goalkeeping coach at Manchester City. Tony Dunne has a golf range in Altrincham. Bill Foulkes lives in Sale. Nobby Stiles is in great demand on the after-dinner circuit. David Sadler has a corporate hospitality business. Bobby Charlton is a director of United and Brian Kidd is a coach at Old Trafford. John Aston has a pet-food shop. Mr Law and Mr Crerand are still there too, playing a bit of golf on company days and that kind of thing.

Our old bosses are no longer with us, or most of them are not: Matt Busby, Jimmy Murphy and our physio, Ted Dalton. Jack Crompton has retired and gone to live in

Pat Crerand: *The passing of a legend – George Best arrives with Denis and myself for the funeral of Sir Matt Busby in 1994.*

Pat Crerand: *There have been several reunions of the 1968 European Cup squad. This time everyone came together for the testimonial game that the club gave me in 1976.*

Tenerife. Wilf McGuinness, who is a lot younger than them of course, is still very busy and works on the after-dinner circuit.

We have an Old Players' Association at Manchester United, and we hold four or five dos a years for charity. The next one is a golf day, for instance, followed by a dinner at Old Trafford. These always have a good turnout with fifty or sixty people sitting down to eat.

The old camaraderie has survived well. One of the greatest things about being a footballer is the fun you have. Someone is always trying something on for a laugh and there is a great feeling of companionship. When Shay Brennan is over, for example, we have this silly ritual where he has to make a grand entrance.

When he first comes in he looks round the room to make sure everyone has noticed him. Then he goes out the door and comes back in again, with more of a flourish this

Above left *David Herd, always a keen club cricketer in Cheshire, teams up with former rugby international Steve Smith.* **Above right** *David Sadler, who now runs his own promotions business.*

time, and we have to clap him in. It's pretty silly but it's one of the things we do, part of the bond between us.

Footballers lead a strange life. It's a short career, punctuated by quite a lot of pain and injury to go with the occasional burst of glory. Not everyone would want to live that way up to the age of about 35, and then find they had to pack it in and do something completely different. There is a lot of insecurity and some people simply do not have the temperament for that.

At Manchester United we have been lucky. It is a great club and it looks after its people extremely well. It is 30 years since we won the European Cup, long before a lot of fans of the Alex Ferguson side were even born. It would be nice if they could win it again – and soon, and make United the top side in Europe once more.

Off to London for a 25th Anniversary reunion dinner in 1993. Front (left to right): Charlton, Aston, Law, Brennan, Dunne, Foulkes, Herd, Stiles. On the steps of the bus: Sadler, Sir Matt, Crerand, Kidd, Stepney.

We both enjoy our golf and play regularly through the summer as part of the Sporting Legends golf team in support of the Wooden Spoon Society charity, Ford's Pat Burch **(right)** suports both the golf team and Wooden Spoon, and **(above)** at the end of another round we both sport our distinctive Wooden Spoon ties with playing partner of the day, company director Geoff Bowles.

1957-58

	P	W	D	L	F	A	Pts
Wolves	42	28	8	6	103	47	64
Preston	42	26	7	9	100	51	59
Tottenham	42	21	9	12	93	77	51
WBA	42	18	14	10	92	70	50
Man City	42	22	5	15	104	100	49
Burnley	42	21	5	16	80	74	47
Blackpool	42	19	6	17	80	67	44
Luton	42	19	6	17	69	63	44
Man United	42	16	11	15	85	75	43
Nottm Forest	42	16	10	16	69	63	42
Chelsea	42	15	12	15	83	79	42
Arsenal	42	16	7	19	73	85	39
Birmingham	42	14	11	17	76	89	39
Aston Villa	42	16	7	19	73	86	39
Bolton	42	14	10	18	65	87	38
Everton	42	13	11	18	65	75	37
Leeds	42	14	9	19	51	63	37
Leicester	42	14	5	23	91	112	33
Newcastle	42	12	8	22	73	81	32
Portsmouth	42	12	8	22	73	88	32
Sunderland	42	10	12	20	54	97	32
Sheff Wed	42	12	7	23	69	92	31

1958-59

	P	W	D	L	F	A	Pts
Wolves	42	28	5	9	110	49	61
Man United	42	24	7	11	103	66	55
Arsenal	42	21	8	13	88	68	50
Bolton	42	20	10	12	79	66	50
WBA	42	18	13	11	88	68	49
West Ham	42	21	6	15	85	70	48
Burnley	42	19	10	13	81	70	48
Blackpool	42	18	11	13	66	49	47
Birmingham	42	20	6	16	84	68	46
Blackburn	42	17	10	15	76	70	44
Newcastle	42	17	7	18	80	80	41
Preston	42	17	7	18	70	77	41
Nottm Forest	42	17	6	19	71	74	40
Chelsea	42	18	4	20	77	98	40
Leeds	42	15	9	18	57	74	39
Everton	42	17	4	21	71	87	38
Luton	42	12	13	17	68	71	37
Tottenham	42	13	10	19	85	95	36
Leicester	42	11	10	21	67	98	32
Man City	42	11	9	22	64	95	31
Aston Villa	42	11	8	23	58	87	30
Portsmouth	42	6	9	27	64	112	21

1959-60

	P	W	D	L	F	A	Pts
Burnley	42	24	7	11	85	61	55
Wolves	42	24	6	12	106	67	54
Tottenham	42	21	11	10	86	50	53
WBA	42	19	11	12	83	57	49
Sheff Wed	42	19	11	12	80	59	49
Bolton	42	20	8	14	59	51	48
Man United	42	19	7	16	102	80	45
Newcastle	42	18	8	16	82	78	44
Preston	42	16	12	14	79	76	44
Fulham	42	17	10	15	73	80	44
Blackpool	42	15	10	17	59	71	40
Leicester	42	13	13	16	66	75	39
Arsenal	42	15	9	18	68	80	39
West Ham	42	16	6	20	75	91	38
Man City	42	17	3	22	78	84	37
Everton	42	13	11	18	73	78	37
Blackburn	42	16	5	21	60	70	37
Chelsea	42	14	9	19	76	91	37
Birmingham	42	13	10	19	63	80	36
Nottm Forest	42	13	9	20	50	74	35
Leeds	42	12	10	20	65	92	34
Luton	42	9	12	21	50	73	30

1960-61

	P	W	D	L	F	A	Pts
Tottenham	42	31	4	7	115	55	66
Sheff Wed	42	23	12	7	78	47	58
Wolves	42	25	7	10	103	75	57
Burnley	42	22	7	13	102	77	51
Everton	42	22	6	14	87	69	50
Leicester	42	18	9	15	87	70	45
Man United	42	18	9	15	88	76	45
Blackburn	42	15	13	14	77	76	43
Aston Villa	42	17	9	16	78	77	43
WBA	42	18	5	19	67	71	41
Arsenal	42	15	11	16	77	85	41
Chelsea	42	15	7	20	98	100	37
Man City	42	13	11	18	79	90	37
Nottm Forest	42	14	9	19	62	78	37
Cardiff	42	13	11	18	60	85	37
West Ham	42	13	10	19	77	88	36
Fulham	42	14	8	20	72	95	36
Bolton	42	12	11	19	58	73	35
Birmingham	42	14	6	22	62	84	34
Blackpool	42	12	9	21	68	73	33
Newcastle	42	11	10	21	86	109	32
Preston	42	10	10	22	43	71	30

1961-62

	P	W	D	L	F	A	Pts
Ipswich	42	24	8	10	93	67	56
Burnley	42	21	11	10	101	67	53
Tottenham	42	21	10	11	88	69	52
Everton	42	20	11	11	88	54	51
Sheff United	42	19	9	14	61	69	47
Sheff Wed	42	20	6	16	72	58	46
Aston Villa	42	18	8	16	65	56	44
West Ham	42	17	10	15	76	82	44
WBA	42	15	13	14	83	67	43
Arsenal	42	16	11	15	71	72	43
Bolton	42	16	10	16	62	66	42
Man City	42	17	7	18	78	81	41
Blackpool	42	15	11	16	70	75	41
Leicester	42	17	6	19	72	71	40
Man United	42	15	9	18	72	75	39
Blackburn	42	14	11	17	50	58	39
Birmingham	42	14	10	18	65	81	38
Wolves	42	13	10	19	73	86	36
Nottm Forest	42	13	10	19	63	79	36
Fulham	42	13	7	22	66	74	33
Cardiff	42	9	14	19	50	81	32
Chelsea	42	9	10	23	63	94	28

1962-63

	P	W	D	L	F	A	Pts
Everton	42	25	11	6	84	42	61
Tottenham	42	23	9	10	111	62	55
Burnley	42	22	10	10	78	57	54
Leicester	42	20	12	10	79	53	52
Wolves	42	20	10	12	93	65	50
Sheff Wed	42	19	10	13	77	63	48
Arsenal	42	18	10	14	86	77	46
Liverpool	42	17	10	15	71	59	44
Nottm Forest	42	17	10	15	67	69	44
Sheff United	42	16	12	14	58	60	44
Blackburn	42	15	12	15	79	71	42
West Ham	42	14	12	16	73	69	40
Blackpool	42	13	14	15	58	64	40
WBA	42	16	7	19	71	79	39
Aston Villa	42	15	8	19	62	68	38
Fulham	42	14	10	18	50	71	38
Ipswich	42	12	11	19	59	78	35
Bolton	42	15	5	22	55	75	35
Man United	42	12	10	20	67	81	34
Birmingham	42	10	13	19	63	90	33
Man City	42	10	11	21	58	102	31
Leyton Orient	42	6	9	27	37	81	21

1963-64

	P	W	D	L	F	A	Pts
Liverpool	42	26	5	11	92	45	57
Man United	42	23	7	12	90	62	53
Everton	42	21	10	11	84	64	52
Tottenham	42	22	7	13	97	81	51
Chelsea	42	20	10	12	72	56	50
Sheff Wed	42	19	11	12	84	67	49
Blackburn	42	18	10	14	89	65	46
Arsenal	42	17	11	14	90	82	45
Burnley	42	17	10	15	71	64	44
WBA	42	16	11	15	70	61	43
Leicester	42	16	11	15	61	58	43
Sheff United	42	16	11	15	61	64	43
Nottm Forest	42	16	9	17	64	68	41
West Ham	42	14	12	16	69	74	40
Fulham	42	13	13	16	58	65	39
Wolves	42	12	15	15	70	80	39
Stoke	42	14	10	18	77	78	38
Blackpool	42	13	9	20	52	73	35
Aston Villa	42	11	12	19	62	71	34
Birmingham	42	11	7	24	54	92	29
Bolton	42	10	8	24	48	80	28
Ipswich	42	9	7	26	56	121	25

1964-65

	P	W	D	L	F	A	Pts
Man United	42	26	9	7	89	39	61
Leeds	42	26	9	7	83	52	61
Chelsea	42	24	8	10	89	54	56
Everton	42	17	15	10	69	60	49
Nottm Forest	42	17	13	12	71	67	47
Tottenham	42	19	7	16	87	71	45
Liverpool	42	17	10	15	67	73	44
Sheff Wed	42	16	11	15	57	55	43
West Ham	42	19	4	19	82	71	42
Blackburn	42	16	10	16	83	79	42
Stoke	42	16	10	16	67	66	42
Burnley	42	16	10	16	70	70	42
Arsenal	42	17	7	18	69	75	41
WBA	42	13	13	16	70	65	39
Sunderland	42	14	9	19	64	74	37
Aston Villa	42	16	5	21	57	82	37
Blackpool	42	12	11	19	67	78	35
Leicester	42	11	13	18	69	85	35
Sheff United	42	12	11	19	50	64	35
Fulham	42	11	12	19	60	78	34
Wolves	42	13	4	25	59	89	30
Birmingham	42	8	11	23	64	96	27

1965-66

	P	W	D	L	F	A	Pts
Liverpool	42	26	9	7	79	34	61
Leeds	42	23	9	10	79	38	55
Burnley	42	24	7	11	79	47	55
Man United	42	18	15	9	84	59	51
Chelsea	42	22	7	13	65	53	51
WBA	42	19	12	11	91	69	50
Leicester	42	21	7	14	80	65	49
Tottenham	42	16	12	14	75	66	44
Sheff United	42	16	11	15	56	59	43
Stoke	42	15	12	15	65	64	42
Everton	42	15	11	16	56	62	41
West Ham	42	15	9	18	70	83	39
Blackpool	42	14	9	19	55	65	37
Arsenal	42	12	13	17	62	75	37
Newcastle	42	14	9	19	50	63	37
Aston Villa	42	15	6	21	69	80	36
Sheff Wed	42	14	8	20	56	66	36
Nottm Forest	42	14	8	20	56	72	36
Sunderland	42	14	8	20	51	72	36
Fulham	42	14	7	21	67	85	35
Northampton	42	10	13	19	55	92	33
Blackburn	42	8	4	30	57	88	20

1966-67

	P	W	D	L	F	A	Pts
Man United	42	24	12	6	84	45	60
Nottm Forest	42	23	10	9	64	41	56
Tottenham	42	24	8	10	71	48	56
Leeds	42	22	11	9	62	42	55
Liverpool	42	19	13	10	64	47	51
Everton	42	19	10	13	65	46	48
Arsenal	42	16	14	12	58	47	46
Leicester	42	18	8	16	78	71	44
Chelsea	42	15	14	13	67	62	44
Sheff United	42	16	10	16	52	59	42
Sheff Wed	42	14	13	15	56	47	41
Stoke	42	17	7	18	63	58	41
WBA	42	16	7	19	77	73	39
Burnley	42	15	9	18	66	76	39
Man City	42	12	15	15	43	52	39
West Ham	42	14	8	20	80	84	36
Sunderland	42	14	8	20	58	72	36
Fulham	42	11	12	19	71	83	34
Southampton	42	14	6	22	74	92	34
Newcastle	42	12	9	21	39	81	33
Aston Villa	42	11	7	24	54	85	29
Blackpool	42	6	9	27	41	76	21

1967-68

	P	W	D	L	F	A	Pts
Man City	42	26	6	10	86	43	58
Man United	42	24	8	10	89	55	56
Liverpool	42	22	11	9	71	40	55
Leeds	42	22	9	11	71	41	53
Everton	42	23	6	13	67	40	52
Chelsea	42	18	12	12	62	68	48
Tottenham	42	19	9	14	70	59	47
WBA	42	17	12	13	75	62	46
Arsenal	42	17	10	15	60	56	44
Newcastle	42	13	15	14	54	67	41
Nottm Forest	42	14	11	17	52	64	39
West Ham	42	14	10	18	73	69	38
Leicester	42	13	12	17	64	69	38
Burnley	42	14	10	18	64	71	38
Sunderland	42	13	11	18	51	61	37
Southampton	42	13	11	18	66	83	37
Wolves	42	14	8	20	66	75	36
Stoke	42	14	7	21	50	73	35
Sheff Wed	42	11	12	19	51	63	34
Coventry	42	9	15	18	51	71	33
Sheff United	42	11	10	21	49	70	32
Fulham	42	10	7	25	56	98	27

1968-69

	P	W	D	L	F	A	Pts
Leeds	42	27	13	2	66	26	67
Liverpool	42	25	11	6	63	24	61
Everton	42	21	15	6	77	36	57
Arsenal	42	22	12	8	56	27	56
Chelsea	42	20	10	12	73	53	50
Tottenham	42	14	17	11	61	51	45
Southampton	42	16	13	13	57	48	45
West Ham	42	13	18	11	66	50	44
Newcastle	42	15	14	13	61	55	44
WBA	42	16	11	15	64	67	43
Man United	42	15	12	15	57	53	42
Ipswich	42	15	11	16	59	60	41
Man City	42	15	10	17	64	55	40
Burnley	42	15	9	18	55	82	39
Sheff Wed	42	10	16	16	41	54	36
Wolves	42	10	15	17	41	58	35
Sunderland	42	11	12	19	43	67	34
Nottm Forest	42	10	13	19	45	57	33
Stoke	42	9	15	18	40	63	33
Coventry	42	10	11	21	46	64	31
Leicester	42	9	12	21	39	68	30
QPR	42	4	10	28	39	95	18